TEACHING ECONOMICS: MORE ALTERNATIVES TO CHALK AND TALK

TEACHING ECONOMICS: MORE ALTERNATIVES TO CHALK AND TALK

Edited by

William E. Becker,
Michael Watts, and
Suzanne R. Becker

Edward Elgar
Cheltenham, UK • Northampton, MA, USA

Published by
Edward Elgar Publishing Limited
Glensanda House
Montpellier Parade
Cheltenham
Glos GL50 1UA
UK

Edward Elgar Publishing, Inc.
136 West Street
Suite 202
Northampton
Massachusetts 01060
USA

A catalogue record for this book
is available from the British Library

Library of Congress Cataloguing in Publication Data
Teaching economics: more alternatives to chalk and talk / edited by William E.
    Becker, Michael Watts, and Suzanne R. Becker
        p. cm.
    Includes bibliographical references and index.
    1. Economics—Study and teaching (Higher) I. Becker, William E. II. Becker,
    Suzanne R., 1946– III. Watts, Michael W.

HB74.5.T427 2006
330'.071'1—dc22   2005051892

ISBN 1 84376 623 X

Printed and bound in Great Britain by MPG Books Ltd, Bodmin, Cornwall

CONTENTS

FIGURES AND TABLES

FIGURES

TABLES

PREFACE

Books on teaching at the post-secondary level have become fashionable as highlighted in the February 11, 2005, *Chronicle of Higher Education* article "Please Take My Advice: 5 Books for Professors who Want to Improve Their Teaching," by Thomas Bartlett. We (Bill Becker and Mike Watts) were fortunate to be in front of this trend with *Teaching Economics to Undergraduates: Alternatives to Chalk and Talk* (Edward Elgar 1998). With this new volume we face the production of a sequel in an environment with many newcomers.

We, and Edward Elgar, were extremely gratified by the reception accorded our 1998 volume (with a paperback edition in 1999) by reviewers and, especially, by paying customers – teachers, departments, and libraries. That is, after all, how sequels come about. We prefer to view this volume as a sequel and not a second edition because it is more of an extension than an update.

In deciding to make this book a true sequel, we recognized that sequels of academic volumes as well as movie and TV sitcom sequels have a nasty habit of failing to live up to the first installment. Nevertheless, we almost immediately decided not to make it a second edition, in which most chapters from the first edition appear with some updates made by the same authors. The main reason for that is simply that most of the chapters in the first volume still stand quite well on their own merits, and have not really aged in any fundamental ways. (Or put differently, we are optimistic enough to hope that people will continue to buy that book, too, perhaps even fueled a bit by the publication of this volume.) On the other hand, there are clearly some methods of delivery, such as using computers and technology in the classroom, and classroom experiments, in which things have changed or expanded so rapidly over the past five years that we did want to offer authors a chance to update their earlier work, or in other cases invite new authors to treat the same topic from a different perspective and experience. In addition, especially in econometrics, game theory, and macroeconomics, the methods of analysis have changed in a manner that cannot be ignored.

One of the most important decisions we made in preparing this sequel was to recognize, explicitly (as always) but on the front cover (for the first time) the vital role Sue Becker has played on this and many other of our publications. Once again, she made the entire book look better, read better, and therefore work better from the sequencing of chapters to the rhetoric employed by chapter authors.

As the grid of Table P.1 shows, five chapters on entirely new topics were commissioned for this volume, leading off with the chapter by Avinash Dixit on game theory. Stephen Buckles and Gail Mitchell Hoyt contributed a totally new chapter on the use of active learning techniques in large lecture classes. Peter Kennedy addresses what should now be taught in the macroeconomics principles class. Martin Shanahan and George Bredon discuss the hot topics associated with distance learning. William Walstad brings us up-to-date on assessment practices.

TABLE P.1: Alternatives (1998) and More Alternatives (2006) to Chalk and Talk

Chapters and Authors in This Volume	Chapters and Authors in 1998 Volume
	Teaching Economics, What Was, Is, and Could Be, by William E. Becker and Michael Watts
Restoring Fun to Game Theory, by Avinash Dixit	
Using Classroom Experiments to Teach Economics, by Denise Hazlett	Student Decision Making as Active Learning: Experimental Economics in the Classroom, by Charles Noussair and James Walker
The Evolution of Cooperative Learning and Economics Instruction, by Robin L. Bartlett	Cooperative Learning, by Robin L. Bartlett
Using the Case Method in the Economics Classroom, by John A. Carlson and Ann Velenchik	Using Cases as an Effective Active Learning Technique, by Stephen Buckles
Using Active Learning Techniques in Large Lecture Classes, by Stephen Buckles and Gail Mitchell Hoyt	
The Macroeconomics Principles Course: What Should be Done, by Peter Kennedy	
Using the Internet and Computer Technology to Teach Economics, by Kim Sosin and William L. Goffe	Using the Internet and Computer Technology to Teach Economics, by Kim Sosin
Teaching and Learning Economics at a Distance, by Martin Shanahan and George Bredon	
Team Term Papers and Presentations, by Michael Watts	Integrating the Practice of Writing Into Economics Instruction, by W. Lee Hansen
Using Nobel Laureates in Economics to Teach Quantitative Methods, by William E. Becker and William H. Greene	Acceptance Speeches by Nobel Laureates in Economics, by William J. Zahka and Engaging Students in Quantitative Analysis with the Academic and Popular Press, by William E. Becker
Assessment of Student Learning in Economics, by William B. Walstad	
	Gender and Active Learning, by Maureen J. Lage and Michael Treglia
	Using Monte Carlo Studies for Teaching Econometrics, by Peter Kennedy
	Using Sports to Teach Economics, by John J. Siegfried and Allen R. Sanderson
	Using Literature and Drama in Undergraduate Economics Courses, by Michael Watts

Robin Bartlett completely reworked her earlier chapter on cooperative learning. Kim Sosin – this time adding William Goffe as a co-author – thoroughly updated and revised her chapter on using computers and technology to teach undergraduate courses in economics.

Four other chapters here deal with topics that were addressed in the first volume, but are written by different authors: Denise Hazlett on classroom experiments, John Carlson and Ann Velenchik on case studies, Michael Watts on writing assignments, and William Becker and William Greene on using Nobel Laureates in economics to teach quantitative methods. To repeat and be as clear about this as we can, in all four of these chapters our intention was not at all to suggest that the related chapters in the first volume are dated or inadequate, but rather that these four topics are both wide and deep enough to warrant additional and different treatments by different authors.

Avinash Dixit, Kim Sosin and William Greene also were invited to present early versions of their work at a conference sponsored by the University of South Australia and the *Journal of Economic Education* on global trends in the teaching of economics. This international conference was held at the University of South Australia in Adelaide Australia in July 2004. Abridged versions of their articles appear in the Summer 2005 proceedings issue of the *Journal of Economic Education*.

There are five chapters in the first volume on topics that are not covered in this volume. Rather than putting those titles and authors in another sentence, perhaps the easiest and clearest way to provide that information and make the point that the two books are, in terms of specific content, more different than they are alike is with the grid of Table P.1, which pairs chapters on the same or very similar topics, and leaves a blank cell to show topics that are treated in one book but not the other.

Only time, reviews, and sales will tell whether we have successfully avoided the sequel curse, but at this point in the publication process we are at least as happy with the general message and specific content in this book as we were with the first volume. It still is not clear whether substantial numbers of academic economists have cut back on chalk and talk in their undergraduate classes since 1998, to engage students more effectively with new teaching methods or course content and examples. We, and many others, have made arguments about why most of them should do that in many other venues, so we won't repeat that here. Instead, the real purpose of this book, and our earlier Elgar volume, is to make it easier for academic economists who want to do that to find ways that work for them and to start using those new approaches. The summary lists of do's and don'ts in each chapter might prevent those who are willing to try a new approach from taking an unnecessary misstep. We believe it is striking that there are few, if any, documented cases of economists who have started using these approaches but then go back to a life of pure chalk and talk, or of their students objecting to less chalk and talk in the classroom.

Finally, we express our thanks to the chapter authors and to the staff at Edward Elgar Publishing but most importantly to Kate Whitsett for her patience, efficiency, and eye for detail in word processing this volume.

William E. Becker
Michael Watts
Suzanne R. Becker
(July 1, 2005)

LIST OF CONTRIBUTORS

Robin L. Bartlett, Professor of Economics, Denison University; Editorial Advisory Board, *Journal of Economic Education*; and Chair, American Economic Association Committee on the Status of Women

Suzanne R. Becker, Assistant Editor, *Journal of Economic Education*

William E. Becker, Professor of Economics, Indiana University; Adjunct Professor, School of Commerce, University of South Australia; Editor, *Journal of Economic Education*; and Editor, *Economic Research Network Educator*

George Bredon, Senior Lecturer, School of Commerce, University of South Australia

Stephen Buckles, Professor of Economics, Vanderbilt University

John A. Carlson, Professor of Economics, School of Management, Purdue University

Avinash Dixit, John J. F. Sherrerd '52 University Professor of Economics, Princeton University

William L. Goffe, Professor of Economics, State University of New York – Oswego

William H. Greene, Professor of Economics, Leonard N. Stern School of Business, New York University

Denise Hazlett, Associate Professor of Economics, Whitman College

Gail Mitchell Hoyt, Associate Professor of Economics, University of Kentucky

Peter E. Kennedy, Professor of Economics, Simon Fraser University; and Associate Editor, *Journal of Economic Education*

Martin Shanahan, Associate Professor, School of Commerce, University of South Australia

Kim Sosin, Professor of Economics and Co-Director of Center for Economic Education, University of Nebraska at Omaha; and Associate Editor, *Journal of Economic Education*

Ann Velenchik, Associate Professor of Economics, Wellesley College

William B. Walstad, John T. and Mabel M. Hay Professor of Economics, College of Business Administration, University of Nebraska – Lincoln; Associate Editor, *Journal of Economic Education*; and Chair, American Economic Association Committee on Economic Education

Michael Watts, Professor of Economics and Director, Center for Economic Education, Purdue University; and Associate Editor, *Journal of Economic Education*

CHAPTER **1**

RESTORING FUN TO GAME THEORY

Avinash Dixit

Game theory starts with an unfair advantage over most other scientific subjects –
it is applicable to numerous interesting and thought-provoking aspects of
decision-making in economics, business, politics, social interactions, and indeed
to much of everyday life, making it automatically appealing to students. However,
too many teachers and textbooks lose this advantage by treating the subject in
such an abstract and formal way that the students' eyes glaze over. Even the
interests of the abstract theorists will be better served if introductory courses are
better motivated using examples and classroom games that engage the students'
interest, and encourage them to go on to more advanced courses. This will create
larger audiences for the abstract game theorists; then they can teach them the
mathematics and the rigor that are surely important aspects of the subject at the
higher levels.

Game theory has become a part of the basic framework of economics, along
with, or even replacing in many contexts, the traditional supply-demand
framework in partial and general equilibrium. Therefore economics students
should be introduced to game theory right at the beginning of their studies.
Teachers of economics usually introduce game theory using economics
applications; Cournot duopoly is the favorite vehicle. However, I prefer a

different approach. Even before anyone is exposed to any economics, everyone has been involved in many strategic games. Undergraduates have played such games with siblings, friends, and parents; strategy is an important aspect of many sports they have played and watched; many movies and books have themes or episodes with game-theoretic content. Following the time-honored principle of teaching that one should start with what the students already know and proceed to build on it, I prefer to teach introductory game theory using examples drawn from such sources.[1] I have found that this approach makes it not only possible, but also productive and enjoyable, to introduce game theory at an elementary level in colleges and even in the better high schools.

In the early days of game theory, even the mathematicians who built up its foundations showed a sense of fun. Von Neumann and Morgenstern expounded mixed strategy equilibria using the story of Sherlock Holmes trying to evade the pursuing Professor Moriarty (1953, pp. 176–178). Williams (1966) gives an exposition of two-person zero-sum minimax theory using many amusing examples, although they verge on the trivial or childish because of the restricted scope. And Tucker's 1950 invention of the story of the prisoner's dilemma (Nasar, 1998, p. 118) was surely a stroke of genius. Most recent theorists have been comparatively humorless, even though they invent amusing names, such as the centipede, horse, or beer-quiche, for their mathematical examples. It is time fun came back to game theory.

I have developed such an elementary course and taught it at Princeton for several years. Susan Skeath has done the same at Wellesley. We have written a textbook, now in its second edition (Dixit and Skeath, 2004) for such a course, comparable in level and style to any introductory or principles textbook in economics, political science, or natural sciences. In this article I offer some teaching ideas and tricks that I have learned from all this experience.

I restrict most of my remarks to the teaching of game theory per se, and not as a part of an economics course. This is because I hold a rather radical view: I believe that an introduction to game theory should precede, not follow, the introductory economics courses in micro and macro. Knowing the concepts of strategy, rollback, and Nash equilibrium unifies many apparently distinct ideas and phenomena in economics. Therefore previous knowledge of elementary game theory will make learning economics easier. For example, if students already know assurance games, Keynesian unemployment becomes a coordination failure leading to a wrong equilibrium selection, rather than a mysterious crossing of two graphs, and many market failures in micro fall into the common framework of the prisoner's dilemma. Also, the view of competition as live interaction of strategies is more appealing to beginners than that of an impersonal adjustment of prices by an invisible hand. Elaboration of this theme of teaching economics game-theoretically merits an article by itself; however, as I said above, I believe that approach to be appropriate for an intermediate level of teaching game theory to economics students, whereas here I focus on the introductory level.

I. GAMES IN CLASS

Playing a few well-designed games in class, and watching others play them, brings to life the concepts of strategy, backward induction, and Nash equilibrium far better than any amount of formal statement or problem-set drill. Indeed, I like to start my game theory course with two classroom games, before teaching or even mentioning any of these concepts at all. The concepts emerge naturally during the discussion of each game.

A Sequential-Move Game

This is a simple Nim-like game. It can be played in many formats, but a particularly attractive one comes from its use in one of the Survivor TV series, namely Episode 6 of Survivor Thailand, which aired in Fall 2002.

There are 21 flags and two players, who alternate in taking turns to remove some flags. At each turn the player has to remove 1, 2, or 3 flags; this is the player's choice at each move. The player who removes the last flag (whether as the sole remaining flag or one of the last surviving set of 2 or 3 flags) is the winner. Instead of using flags, you can use coins; lay them out on the glass of the overhead projector so the whole class can easily see what is going on.

In the Survivor show, the game was played as an "immunity challenge" between two teams, called "tribes." The losing tribe had to vote out one of its members, weakening it for future competitions. In the specific context, this loss had a crucial effect on the eventual outcome of the game. Thus a million-dollar prize hinged on the ability to do the simple calculation. A video clip of the competition is available from the web site for the show, <http://www.cbs.com/primetime/survivor5/show/episode06/s5story.shtml>. If you have the right kind of equipment available in the classroom, you can download and show the clip "More Action at the Immunity Challenge" available from page 5 of this site. The actual players got almost all of their moves wrong, so seeing it first and then playing a similar game themselves will be a good way for your students to learn the concepts.

The correct solution is simple. If you leave the other player (or team) with four flags, he must remove 1, 2, or 3, and then you can take the rest and win. To make sure of leaving the other player with four flags, at the turn before you have to leave him facing eight flags. Carrying the logic further, that means leaving 12, 16, and 20. Therefore starting with 21 flags, the first player should remove one, and then proceed to take four minus whatever the other takes at his immediately preceding turn.

The first time a pair of students play this game, they make choices almost at random. After their game is over, watched by the whole class, choose two others. They do better than the first pair; they figure out one or perhaps even two of the final rounds correctly. By the third or at most the fourth time, the players will have figured out the full backward induction.

Then hold a brief discussion. You should nudge or guide it a little toward three conclusions. First, the idea of backward induction, or the importance of solving sequential-move games backward from the final moves. Second, the idea of "correct strategies" that constitute a solution of the game. Tell them that it will soon be given a formal name, rollback equilibrium. Finally, the idea that one can learn correct strategies by actually playing a game. With this comes the idea that if a game is played by experienced players, we might expect to observe correct strategies and equilibrium outcomes. This will give the students some confidence in the concepts of backward induction and rollback equilibrium.

The last remark motivates a brief digression. Over the last decade, behavioral game theorists have made a valuable contribution to the stock of interesting games that can be played in classrooms. However, many of them come to the subject with a negative agenda, namely to argue that everything in conventional game theory is wrong. My own experience suggests otherwise. To be sure, it takes time and experience merely to understand the rules of any game, and a lot of practice and experimentation to play it well. But students learn quite fast. Advanced researchers delight in the difficulties of learning, and on how actual outcomes can differ from the equilibrium predictions. But it is counterproductive to give the impression to beginners that what they are about to learn is all wrong; it destroys their whole motivation to learn. I find it better to convey a sense of guarded optimism about the standard Nash theory, without pretending that it closes the subject. Of course I believe this to be the truth of the matter.

A Simultaneous-Move Game

My second game is a version of the famous "generalized beauty contest." Choose 10 students in the class, and give them blank cards. Each student is to write his or her name on the card, and a number between 0 and 100. The cards will be collected and the numbers on them averaged. The student whose choice is closest to half of the average is the winner. These rules are of course explained in advance and in public.

The Nash equilibrium of this game is 0. In fact it results from an iterated dominance argument. Because the average can never exceed 100, half of the average can never exceed 50. Therefore any choice above 50 is dominated by 50. Then the average can never exceed 50, ... The first time the game is played, the winner is usually close to 25. This fits Nagel's (1995) observation that the outcome is as if the students expect the others to choose at random, averaging 50, and then choose half of that. Next choose a different set of 10 students from the class (who have watched the outcome of the first group's game). This second group chooses much smaller numbers, and the winner is close to 10 (as if one more round of the dominance calculation was performed) or even 5 or 6 (as if two more rounds were performed). The third group of 10 chooses much smaller numbers, including several zeros, and the winner's choice is as low as 3 or 4. Incidentally, I have found that learning proceeds somewhat faster by watching others play than when the same group of 10 plays successively. Perhaps the brain does a better job of observation and interpretation if the ego is not engaged in playing the game.

Again hold a brief discussion. The points to bring out are: (1) The logical concept of dominance, iterated elimination of dominated strategies, and the culmination in a Nash equilibrium. (2) Getting close to the Nash equilibrium by the experience of playing the game. Whether it is a crucial flaw of the theory that 0 is rarely exactly attained, or the theory gives a good approximation, can be a point to be debated depending on the time available. (3) The idea that if you have good reason to believe that others will not be playing their Nash equilibrium strategies, then your optimal choice will also differ from your own Nash equilibrium strategy.

The discussion can also touch on the question: what if the object is to come closest to the average, not half of the average. That game is of course Keynes' famous metaphor for the stock market, where everyone is trying to guess what everyone else is trying to guess. The game has multiple Nash equilibria, each sustained by its own bootstraps. Details of this are best postponed to a later point in the course when you cover multiple equilibria more systematically, but a quick mention in the first class provides the students an interesting economic application at the outset. You can also stress the importance of this game in their own lives. Part or even all of their retirement funds are likely to be in individual accounts. When they decide how to invest this sum, they will have to think through the question: Will the historical pattern of returns and volatility of various assets persist when everyone makes the same decisions that I am now contemplating? This interaction between individual choice (strategy) and aggregate outcomes (equilibrium) comes naturally to someone who is trained to think game-theoretically, but others are often liable to forget the effect of everyone's simultaneous choices. In the context of saving for retirement this can be very costly.

All-Pay Auction

In later classes I play several other games, such as the centipede and ultimatum games, and of course several variants of prisoners' dilemmas and collective action games, each of which illustrates a basic theoretical concept or some way in which the experience of reality departs from the theory. An amusing climax I have tried in the very last class is the "applause auction." Princeton has a tradition that at the end of your last lecture in each course you get a brief polite round of applause. At this point I offer a reward, usually $20 but sometimes as much as $50, to the person who continuously applauds the longest. This is an all-pay auction; the students are bidding in kind, namely applause, and all bidders pay their bids, win or lose.

Most students drop out within the first 15 or 20 minutes, but a few last absurdly long. The record to date is where three students lasted four and one-half hours. To complete the educational purpose of the game (and to avoid the risk of a headline "Professor Buys Applause" in the student newspaper) I send an e-mail to the class explaining the game. I point out that all-pay auctions are quite common: the contestants in sporting competitions or elections spend their time, efforts, and money, with no refunds for the losers. Such contests can escalate, and the nuclear arms race was a classic example of "overbidding." I refer them to Hirshleifer and Riley (1992, ch. 10) and Bulow and Klemperer (1999) for the theory of such games. And I tell them about any interesting special occurrences in that year's competition. One year, for example, six people remained, and were discussing splitting the prize. Five agreed, but one refused. At that point the other five got angry and threatened to stay as long as necessary to outlast the sixth. After a few minutes of experiencing the credibility of this threat, the sixth gave up, and then the other five stopped simultaneously to share the prize. This was a nice example of people's instinctive willingness to punish anti-social behavior even at a personal cost (Fehr and Gächter, 2000).

The combined experience of teachers of game theory is gradually building up a good collection of classroom games. Another recent example is Brokaw and Merz (2004).

Role-Playing

Games where the class is split into teams that play different roles in acting out a strategic situation can be very instructive. I have run such sessions, for example one where terrorists or bank robbers have taken hostages and the authorities are negotiating for their release, and another on negotiation for peace in the Middle East. I assign some general background reading, but otherwise leave the students to devise their own agendas and strategies. I find that they take these exercises seriously, and think hard and well. The Middle East peace negotiation is a case in point. The students devised imaginative and realistic strategies. The Israeli delegation did not show up, but instead sent a declaration saying they would not negotiate until the violence ended. The Palestinian delegation showed up with good intentions, but could not credibly promise to control their extreme factions. Finally, the extremist group pulled out water pistols and held everyone hostage! The United Nations delegation should have thought of this and posted guards at the door to check backpacks.

As I give the students a lot of freedom, I have to think ahead and be ready for a large number of alternative scenarios that could develop, but on occasion I have been pleasantly surprised by the students' ideas. Other teachers may prefer a somewhat tighter structure; still the role playing exercise will be beneficial.

Computer Games: the Wild-West Shootout

Finally, it is possible to program more elaborate games on a computer network. Numerous games of this kind are readily available; Charles Holt of the University of Virginia offers an excellent collection of web-based games on his web site, <http://www.people.virginia.edu/~cah2k/teaching.html>. Vesna Prasnikar of Carnegie-Mellon University has software called Comlabgames, and Paul Romer's web-based educational materials company Aplia <http://www.aplia.com> markets game-playing software. However, I find that many such games are too abstract – they offer matrices or trees to which payoffs can be added and the students are asked to take the row or column roles. I prefer ones with context and appeal, better related to the kinds of computer games students will have played before.

My best such game is a four-person, three-bullet duel. (You could name the game "The Good, the Bad, the Bold, and the Beautiful.") Students in the class are seated at terminals in the computer cluster, and randomly matched into foursomes. Each person in a foursome sees on his/her screen a square divided into four quadrants; this is schematically reproduced in Figure 1.1. Each player starts with three bullets, and (as long as he/she is still "alive" in the game) can shoot at any of the others at any time. To shoot at a player, you move your cursor into the intended victim's quadrant and click on your left mouse button. The probability of scoring a hit increases with time, and this is indicated by the shrinkage of a central square that overlaps the four quadrants. At any time, the probability of hitting an adjacent player is higher than that of hitting the diagonally opposite player. The formulas for the increases in probabilities are announced in the rules handed out at the beginning. The total shrinkage time is two minutes. Your score in any one such play equals the number of seconds you stay alive, plus a bonus of 50 points if you are alive at the end of the two minutes, and an additional bonus of 100 points if you are the only player in your foursome to remain alive at the end of the two minutes (to discourage collusion where no one shoots).

This is played several times, with varying matches, so that there are no repeated foursomes. Indeed, the identity of the others in one's foursome in any one play is not made known. Each student's score for the session is the average over all the games he/she plays. This forms a small part of the course credit, so the stakes are quite high.

Time remaining = 85 seconds

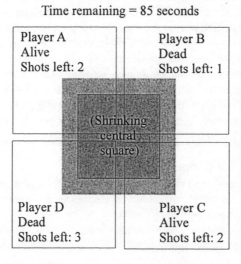

FIGURE 1.1: Four-person, three-bullet duel.

There are also sets of repetitions under different information conditions. In the first, every player knows whether each of the others is alive or dead and the number of bullets they have left; this is the condition shown Figure 1.1. In the second, each player knows whether the others are alive or dead, but not the number of bullets they have left; thus the last of the three information lines does not appear in this set of repetitions. In the third, the players do not even know whether the others are alive or dead; this is as if they are hiding behind a building or a tree in an actual wild-west shootout.

As far as I know, this game has no analytical solution. My observation from the classroom performance is that reasonably patient strategies do well, and that less patience is slightly better in the later limited information conditions, but that most students are too impatient, and shoot too many bullets too quickly. I have also tried sessions of the game accompanied by suitably tense music (the Bolero, or the James Bond theme), and found, as expected, that this leads to itchier fingers on the trigger. Playing this game several times and in different information conditions gives the students a good hands-on way of learning how to develop heuristics for games in which the calculation of Nash equilibrium is too difficult. (See Simon and Schaeffer, 1992; Dixit and Skeath, 2004, section 3.5B, for a discussion of chess from this perspective.)

This game has its counterparts in economics and business. The general idea is that you face a tradeoff between shooting late to increase the probability of scoring a hit, and shooting early to reduce the risk of getting shot by someone else. This is the same situation that firms in high-technology industries face when they are deciding when to introduce a new product – wait to make it more perfect, or rush to be first in the market? The game gives students an interesting hands-on experience of the calculation and the tension involved in such decisions.

The code for the game is specific to Princeton's computer cluster system, but if you want to implement the game in your own institution, any competent computer science major should be able to write the code for your cluster during the summer between his/her junior and senior years. I have implemented two other games – a prisoner's dilemma and a bargaining game – and can supply similar information about them on request for teachers who want to get them programmed at their schools.

Do's and Don'ts for Classroom Games

- Do use real money for prizes. Even small amounts raise student interest and attention. You can make the students' scores in the game count for a small fraction of the course credit.
- Do use games with stories, not just abstract trees or matrices.
- Do follow each game immediately with a discussion that brings out the general concepts or methods of analysis that the game was supposed to illustrate. If there isn't enough time for a good discussion, circulate an explanation or post it on the course web site.
- Don't make the game so complex that the main conceptual point is smothered.

- Don't choose games where the outcome depends significantly on uncertainty rather than skill, especially if the games count toward the course credit.
- Do allow enough independent repetitions for any effects of chance to be reduced by averaging, if chance is involved.

II. MOVIES AND TV SHOWS

Many movies contain scenes that illustrate some aspect of strategic interaction. You can screen these scenes in class as an introduction to that topic, and let a discussion lead on to theoretical analysis of it.

Nash Equilibrium
One cannot ask for a better movie to get students to improve their understanding of this basic concept of game theory than *A Beautiful Mind,* which was based, however loosely, on the life of John Nash himself, and in turn on Nasar's (1998) biography which, although it emphasized the psychological and mental aspects, gave a correct account of the Nash equilibrium concept. The crucial scene from the movie, where Nash is supposed to have discovered his concept of equilibrium, shows him in a bar with three male friends. A blonde and her four brunette friends walk in. All four men would like to win the blonde's favor. But if they all approach her, each will stand at best a one-fourth chance; actually the movie seems to suggest that she would reject all four. The men will have to turn to the brunettes, but then the brunettes will reject them also, because "no one likes to be second choice." The movie Nash says that the solution is for them all to ignore the blonde and go for the brunettes. One of the other men thinks this is just a ploy on Nash's part to get the others to go for the brunettes so he can be the blonde's sole suitor. And if you think about the situation game-theoretically, the movie Nash is wrong and the friend is right. The strategy profile where all men go for the brunettes is not a Nash equilibrium: given the strategies of the others, any one of them gains by deviating and going for the blonde. In fact Anderson and Engers (2002) show that the game has multiple equilibria, but the only outcome that cannot be a Nash equilibrium is the supposedly brilliant solution found by the movie Nash!

Mixed Strategies
The concept of mixed strategies is often initially counterintuitive. Although there are many situations in sports that serve to introduce it, I like one scene from *The Princess Bride,* a whimsical comedy that has the added advantage of being a teenage favorite movie. In this scene, the hero (Westley) challenges one of the villains (Vizzini) to a duel of wits. Westley will poison one of two wine cups without Vizzini observing his action, and set one in front of each of them. Vizzini will decide which cup he will drink from; Westley then must drink from the other cup. Vizzini goes through a whole sequence of arguments as to why Westley

would or would not choose to poison the one cup or the other. Finally he believes he knows which cup is safe, and drinks from it. Westley drinks from the other. Just as Vizzini is laughing and advising Westley to "never go against a Sicilian when death is on the line," Vizzini drops dead.

Pause the videotape or disc at this point and have a brief discussion. The students will quickly see that each of Vizzini's arguments is inherently self-contradictory. If Westley thinks through to the same point that leads Vizzini to believe that a particular cup will contain the poison, he should instead put the poison in the other cup. Any systematic action can be thought through and defeated by the other player. Therefore the only correct strategy is to be unsystematic or random.

Asymmetric Information

Actually this is not the main point of the story. Resume the tape or disc. The princess is surprised to find that Westley had put the poison in the cup he placed closer to himself. "They were both poisoned," he replies, "I have been building up immunity to Iocaine for years." Thus the game being played was really one of asymmetric information; Vizzini did not know Westley's payoffs, and did not think the strategy of poisoning both cups was open to him. At this point you can show a clip from another movie classic, *Guys and Dolls*. Sky Masterson recalls the advice from his father: "Son, no matter how far you travel, or how smart you get, always remember this: Some day, somewhere, a guy is going to come to you and show you a nice brand-new deck of cards on which the seal is never broken, and this guy is going to offer to bet you that the jack of spades will jump out of this deck and squirt cider in your ear. But son, do not bet him, for as sure as you do you are going to get an ear full of cider." (The cited text is from Runyon 1933 [1992].)

Brinkmanship

Many movies have scenes that deal with the question of how to get some vital information that only your adversary possesses, because he knows that the threat of killing him is not credible. The situation plays out differently in *High Wind in Jamaica, Crimson Tide, The Maltese Falcon,* and *The Gods Must Be Crazy.* You can show excerpts from all four, and then hold a discussion to compare and contrast them.

In *High Wind in Jamaica,* the pirate captain Chavez (the information-seeker) backs off and tries a different approach. In *Crimson Tide,* the U.S. Navy submarine captain Ramsey threatens to kill a co-conspirator of the person who has the crucial firing codes for the submarine's missiles. This works: the person gives up the code. The conspirators were trying to prevent the start of a possibly unnecessary nuclear war in which millions would die, but it is interesting that the immediate death of someone you know can weigh more in your calculation than abstract megadeaths.

In *The Maltese Falcon,* the hero Samuel Spade (played by Humphrey Bogart) is the only person who knows where the priceless gem-studded falcon is hidden, and the chief villain Caspar Gutman (Sydney Greenstreet) is threatening him for this information. This produces a classic exchange, here cited from the book (Hammett, 1930) but reproduced almost verbatim in the movie.

> Spade flung his words out with a brutal sort of carelessness that gave them more weight than they could have got from dramatic emphasis or from loudness. "If you kill me, how are you going to get the bird? If I know you can't afford to kill me till you have it, how are you going to scare me into giving it to you?"
>
> Gutman cocked his head to the left and considered these questions. His eyes twinkled between puckered lids. Presently he gave his genial answer: "Well, sir, there are other means of persuasion besides killing and threatening to kill."
>
> "Sure," Spade agreed. "but they're not much good unless the threat of death is behind them to hold the victim down. See what I mean? If you try something I don't like I won't stand for it. I'll make it a matter of your having to call it off or kill me, knowing you can't afford to kill me."
>
> "I see what you mean." Gutman chuckled. "That is an attitude, sir, that calls for the most delicate judgment on both sides, because, as you know, sir, men are likely to forget in the heat of action where their best interests like and let their emotions carry them away."
>
> Spade too was all smiling blandness. "That's the trick, from my side," he said, "to make my play strong enough that it ties you up, but yet not make you mad enough to bump me off against your better judgment."

The class discussion can explore the nature of these strategies. The scene can be seen as an example of Schelling's idea of the (strategic) rationality of (seeming) irrationality (1960, pp. 17–18); Gutman is making his threat credible by pointing out that he may act irrationally. But it is better seen as an example of the dynamic game of brinkmanship (Schelling, 1960, ch. 8; 1966, ch. 3). Both parties by persisting in their actions – Gutman in his torture, and Spade in his defiance – are raising the risk that Gutman may get mad and do something against his own rational interest. Each is exploring the risk-tolerance of the other, in the hope that it is lower than his own risk-tolerance so that the other will "blink first." A more formal analysis of this in the context of the Cuban missile crisis is in Dixit and Skeath (2004, ch. 14).

The scene from *The Gods Must Be Crazy* makes this escalation of risk more explicit. An assassination attempt on the dictator of an African country has failed, and one of the team of gunmen has been captured. He is being interrogated for the location of the group's headquarters and the leader. The scene is the inside of a helicopter. The blindfolded gunman is standing with his back to the open door. Above the noise of the rotors, the army officer questions the gunman a couple of times, and gets only shakes of the head. Then he simply pushes the gunman out the door. The scene switches to the outside of the helicopter, which we now see is just barely hovering above the ground, and the gunman has fallen six feet on to his back. The army officer appears at the door and says, "The next time it will be a little bit higher."

Brinkmanship arises in many economic contexts, most notably that of wage bargaining where the risk of a strike or a lockout increases as protracted negotiations fail to produce results. Understanding the subtleties and the risks of this strategy is therefore an important part of an economist's education, and these movie scenes illustrate it in memorable ways.

Dr. Strangelove

This is a universal favorite strategic movie; it illustrates many issues of commitments, threats, and promises, all within a compelling narrative full of tension and satirical humor. Two scenes in the Pentagon war room are essential viewing: (1) Where the U.S. president Merkin Muffley hears how General Ripper has made irreversible his unauthorized launching of a nuclear attack on the Soviet Union by cutting off all communication with his base and with the aircraft. (2) Where Dr. Strangelove explains why the doomsday machine is such a credible deterrent. When the President asks, "But how is it possible for the machine to be triggered automatically and yet impossible to de-trigger?" Strangelove replies: "Mr. President, it is not only possible; it is essential. That is the whole idea." Then he asks the Soviet ambassador: "But the whole point of the machine is lost if you keep it a secret. Why didn't you tell the world?"

There are numerous other incidents in the movie that illustrate other points of strategy, and a good case can be made for screening the whole movie and discussing it. However, the whole context of the cold war may be too dated for today's students, and they may find the whole period atmosphere – the black-and-white film, the sexist jokes – unappealing. With a little prior explanation of the context and warnings that the offensive-sounding bits are satirical, my students have enjoyed the movie, except that a large fraction of them, brainwashed by Hollywood, to the last minute expect a happy ending where somehow the plane would be recalled. For those of you who want to try such a screening and discussion, a report on the post-movie discussion that I circulated to my class is attached as Appendix 1.A.

These movies are just a few of the large collection that is available; I am sure other teachers have their own different favorites. Television can also be a good source. Trandel (1999) offers an early example from a game show. Many episodes of the BBC sitcoms *Yes, Minister* and *Yes, Prime Minister* are outstanding lessons in strategy: bargaining, commitment, signaling and screening. Unfortunately the setting is too unfamiliar to non-British students, and the period is also getting dated for many of them, even though it is barely 10 to 20 years ago. Finally, in the very first of the CBS Survivor series, the eventual winner Richard Hatch used a clever "losing to win" strategy to get to the final twosome. This is too lengthy to explain here, but the scene is available from the CBS web site <http://www.cbs.com/primetime/survivor/show/episode13/story.shtml>; the immunity challenge when three players are left is the crucial scene. A game-theoretic analysis is in Dixit and Skeath (2004, section 3.7).

Do's and Don'ts for Movie Screenings

- Do take suggestions from students about other movies or games you can use – their ideas are more likely to be appealing to other students than yours, which may date back a few years and therefore may be unfamiliar and uninteresting to today's students. But ask and discuss in advance just what strategic issue the excerpt illustrates. Enlist their help in acquiring tapes.

- Do come prepared with your videotapes wound to the exact point you want to start. If you need to show two or more disjoint excerpts from the same movie, bring the appropriate number of copies of the tape, each cued to the right place. If you are using DVDs, make a note of the exact time (minutes and seconds) where your excerpt begins, and practice ahead of time how to start the DVD quickly at the right point. If the students have to wait while you find the right place or the right button, or while you wind the tape to the next starting point, this distracts their attention, and loses effectiveness of movie or TV clips.

- Don't assume that students know the general plots of the movies from which you show excerpts. Prepare a brief explanation of the situation and the characters as it pertains to your excerpt, and give it just before you start the videotape.

- Don't show a whole movie or a long clip when only a small point pertains to strategy. The students will get distracted by too many of the other incidental aspects.

III. LITERATURE

Novels and short stories are an even richer collection of illustrations of strategies in action. *Les Liaisons Dangereuses* must be an unmatched source for analyzing issues of credibility, and of private information about motives (players' types). Historical literature also has valuable insights; Thucydides' *The Peloponnesian War* recounts debates and speeches that have outstanding expositions of strategic themes. In Shakespeare's *Henry V*, the famous speech before the battle of Agincourt is an excellent example of incentives to motivate soldiers to fight; see the discussion in Dixit and Nalebuff (1991, pp. 161–163). And *Othello* is full of strategic issues.

Many novels of crime and detection, with their themes of information and betrayal, are also excellent sources for illustrating these ideas. My personal favorite is *Cogan's Trade* by Higgins (1974). In it, the Boston mafia protected a high-stakes poker game. The person (named Trattman) who ran the game himself arranged for it to be robbed. But by the time the mafia bosses found this out, all the fuss had died down, and Trattman was well-liked, so they did nothing. But then some others got the idea that if they robbed the game, Trattman would be the automatic suspect and they would escape detection. The mafia bosses discover the truth, but they face a bigger problem – their reputation as effective protectors has been ruined and must be rebuilt. For this they need a signaling strategy, and to make it credible in the standard Spencian manner, the signal has to be carried to excess, in this instance literally to overkill. Cogan, the up-and-coming enforcer, explains the argument very clearly and explicitly to the consiglieri (Higgins, 1974, ch. 8):

> "It's his responsibility," Cogan said, "He did it before and he lied before and he fooled everybody, and I said … 'They should've whacked him out before.' … Now it happened again. It's his responsibility for what the guys think." …
> "He didn't do it," the driver said. "Not this time, anyway."
> "That's not what everybody knows," Cogan said. "Shit, we're gonna have kids waiting in line, [to] knock them fuckin' games over, they open up again. … If he gets away with this, well, we might just as well forget it, once and for all, and just quit. … Tell [the godfather], ask him, where the guys come from, in the game. … They're not gonna come in, is all. Trattman did it before, [they think] Trattman did it again. … Trattman's gotta be hit."

When he gets the godfather's go-ahead to execute the overkill strategy of whacking out everyone involved (including Trattman), Cogan forms a temporary alliance with one of the miscreants in the second robbery, to get his cooperation in setting up another for the hit. But the ally fails to think through the game, and to solve it backward. Therefore he does not realize that Cogan's promise to spare him is not credible. Of course Cogan knows perfectly well what is going to happen: he responds to the consiglieri's question when outlining his plan for the hit (Higgins 1974, ch. 16): "Will he be all right?" … "For a while. Not long, but a while." This instance of the life-and-death importance of doing backward induction correctly is another useful lesson to emphasize from the novel.

Watts (2003) is an excellent compendium of excerpts from the literature bearing on economics. Some of them have game-theoretic content; for example the excerpt from *The Perfect Storm* explains the prisoner's dilemma that leads to depletion of a fishery, and that from *The Merchant of Venice* has brilliant lessons about commitment and interpretation of an incompletely specified contract. Rasmusen (2000) includes some game-theoretic stories and cartoons in his collection of simpler articles on the subject. But a game-theory equivalent of Watts' large economics anthology is eagerly awaited.

Pending such a collection, I have found that any substantial use of literature in today's game theory courses is problematic, because it requires the students to do too much reading. If the Harry Potter novels had good strategic components, the problem might be solved. But unfortunately the rules of the game in those books are hidden and keep changing somewhat randomly, making them poorly suited for illustrating game-theoretic ideas. If you are fortunate enough to have students who are well-read or willing to read extensively for the course, you will get many good suggestions for the use of literature in your courses from Brams (1994).

IV. CONCLUDING REMARKS

Imaginative use of game-playing, movies, literature, and such other illustrations makes game theory much more fun to teach and to learn. This can be done without sacrificing any rigor. The ancillary material supplements and elucidates the theory; it does not supplant theory. And although I have barely touched on specific applications to teaching economics, I hope the few I have mentioned suggest to you numerous other ways to enrich that part of your teaching also. In short, I believe this approach is a recipe to make everyone better off – an all-too-rare instance of a feasible Pareto improvement. The suggestions offered in this chapter should inspire some of you to develop and teach courses of this kind.

APPENDIX 1.A: Guide To Strategies in *Dr. Strangelove*

What follows is a statement and discussion of the many strategic issues and incidents from the movie. For more general information about the movie itself, consult its special web site, <http://www.filmsite.org/drst.html>, or its page from the Internet Movie Database web site, <http://us.imdb.com/Title?0057012>.

Plan R

The reason for creating Plan R was that the under the previous procedures the U.S. nuclear deterrent was not "credible": if a sneak Soviet attack killed the President, there would be no one to order a U.S. nuclear retaliation. This sense of lack of credibility is different from the one used in game theory, namely that the U.S. president, if left free to choose after a Soviet attack, would not want to unleash retaliation. The difference is between the *ability* and the *will* to act. In ordinary language the two senses are often confused, and here the official explaining the position to President Muffley uses it in the "ability" sense. You should be aware of the distinction, and in the context of this course, and of game theory more generally, should use it only in the "will" sense.

In strategic terms, the plan improved our "second strike capability" – the ability to retaliate after being subjected to a first strike. If both sides have better second strike capability, the nuclear balance is safer because neither has the temptation to launch a preemptive first strike, and neither feels the need to do so because of a perception or fear that the other side might launch a preemptive first strike. But the plan seems to have been a secret; even the President was unaware of it. Its existence should have been better publicized. Certainly the Soviets should have been informed, to make it clear to them that a sneak attack that destroyed Washington and killed the President would avail them nothing.

The plan failed because it did not have effective safeguards to prevent a lower-echelon commander from launching an uncalled-for attack; the plan was too risky. Any plan of this kind has a tradeoff between effectiveness and safety, including some of the middle ways: (1) The authority vests with a group of military commanders, perhaps at different bases, and say three out of five Go commands are needed. (Allowing any one of the five to give the go-code is too unsafe; requiring unanimity is too ineffective.) Or the code could be in two or more parts. Similar controls exist in some systems for the actual launching of missiles, where two people must turn keys simultaneously. (2) The ability to issue the go-code could be conditioned on some objective event, for example a sufficiently high level of radiation in the United States. (3) The planes could be required to obtain confirmation of the go-code from a different base than the one that issued the initial order. (4) The system could use automatic instead of human pilots. But these would have been less effective in real war – they would not have saved the plane with heroics after the missile attack.

To allow the President to retrieve the situation after an unprovoked launch of Plan R, there could be an overriding recall code, or a second radio receiver controlled directly from the Pentagon. The risk of destruction of the plane's receiver circuits could be handled by requiring that the mission be aborted if the CRM-114 is not functional. But this may err on the side of too little effectiveness – that mission may be essential to the United States. (Compare the situation and conflict in the movie *Crimson Tide*.)

The Soviet Union actually had something very like Plan R, but with various human and mechanical safeguards. It was (wrongly) called "Russia's Doomsday Machine" (Blair, 1993).

General Ripper's Attack

To commit the U.S. officially to his attack, Ripper hijacked several elements of Plan R itself: (1) He sealed off the base, cut off communications and impounded radios. (2) He sent a phone message and was then unavailable for further discussions or questions. (3) He sent the go-code when the planes were already at fail-safe so they would not need a further authorization. (4) He kept the recall code secret, and finally killed himself (the ultimate irreversible commitment) rather than risk revealing it under torture.

He put the President and the general staffs under great time pressure, and reckoned that it would compel them to back him up with an all-out attack. In the war-room meeting, General Turgidson supported this course of action, as it would yield a less bad post-war environment: "only" 10 to 20 million dead.

There were flaws in Ripper's strategy: (1) He did not reckon that the President would refuse to launch an all-out attack, and would instead contact the Soviet Premier and even help the Soviets shoot down the planes. (2) The base was not perfectly sealed: Mandrake discovered a working radio playing music, and later a pay phone (and a Coke machine to supply coins!). (3) The base defenses were overcome very quickly. (4) Ripper's obsessive doodling enabled Mandrake to guess the recall code.

The Doomsday Machine

The important features of the Doomsday Machine were: (1) It threatened a very dire consequence, namely destruction of all human and animal life on earth, to serve as a deterrent. (2) It was automatic, making it credible as a commitment to actions that "no sane man would take." Its crucial flaw: It was kept a secret. The Soviets should not only have announced it as soon as it was operational, but also invited U.S. officials to inspect it.

Would this have deterred Ripper? If he was truly concerned about the purity of the American people's precious bodily fluids, he would not have wanted them to be destroyed by radioactivity. But if this was just a symptom of some underlying psychosis, who knows what he might do.

Given the risk of "errors," the doomsday machine is too large a threat. Besides the "error" that occurred in the movie, such a machine might be triggered by mistake (or a runaway computer as in the movie *War Games*), or by a "very small" attack. It might also prove too unpopular with the U.S. public. As Dr. Strangelove explains to President Muffley, for just such reasons the U.S. had decided not to build such a device.

A doomsday machine could be made safer by programming it to react only to a "large enough" attack, but that would make it vulnerable to "salami tactics": repeated attacks each of which is too small to trigger it. The machine could be made probabilistic like Russian roulette, but this concept might be too difficult to explain to the public or even the opposing military chiefs. And if a human override is introduced, the crucial automatic nature is lost.

A country might announce that it has a doomsday machine without actually building one. It could even construct Wizard-of-Oz-like appearances – computers etc. – but leave out the actual bombs. This might be a very effective deterrent. But in the U.S. there might be adverse public reaction to the announcement of the installation. Moreover, if say an investigative reporter found out the truth, that might jeopardize the credibility of our real deterrents.

The Phone Conversation

President Merkin Muffley used various devices to convince Premier Kissoff that he was sincere and was not launching a massive attack: (1) He brought the Soviet ambassador into the highly confidential war room, showed him the full situation, and had him talk to the Premier first. (2) He pointed out that if he had meant to launch a sneak attack he would have done so without calling first, so the very act of making the phone call was a credible signal of his good intentions: "If it wasn't a friendly call, you would never even have got it." Of course the Soviets might still retain a suspicion that he intended to misdirect their attention on defending the stated targets while the real U.S. attack came elsewhere, but ... (3) The Soviets' trust was reinforced when the locations of the planes were correctly revealed, some were shot down, and others recalled.

But all this was defeated by the cowboy pilot's "initiative," namely, his decision to bomb an unauthorized target. Possible ways of avoiding this risk are: (1) Have a general rule that the bomb cannot be dropped other than on the specified primary or secondary targets. (2) Not give the pilot the coordinates of any other targets. In the movie he could have got those from the profile envelopes for all the other attack plans, but these days one could transmit the plans electronically very fast with the initial go order itself. (3) The Soviets should not have focused *all* their forces on that one location, to guard against just such a mishap, or even more important, against deliberate U.S. cheating. (4) There could be a device located in each plane to destroy it in just such an emergency on an electronic command from the U.S. But if the Soviets learned the destruction signal they would have a surefire defense. Also, the knowledge that such a device existed would seriously lower the morale of U.S. aircrews. Again, there is a tradeoff between risk and effectiveness, and there is no truly ideal solution.

NOTES

* This chapter was presented at the University of South Australia and *Journal of Economic Education* conference: "What We Teach and How We Teach It - Perspectives on Economics from Around the Globe," July 14-16 2004, Adelaide, Australia. I thank William Becker for comments on a preliminary draft.
[1] If the instructor introduced the prisoner's dilemma by developing a Cournot duopoly game, the students would have to learn two new things simultaneously. If the instructor asks "Why do shared dorm rooms usually become very untidy?" students know the temptation to shirk from a familiar context, and can easily tie it to the temptation to cut prices in duopoly, and then to the formal concepts of dominant strategies and the dilemma.

REFERENCES

Anderson, S., and M. Engers. 2002. A beautiful blonde: A Nash coordination game. University of Virginia, working paper, <http://www.virginia.edu/economics/papers/engers/abb.PDF>

Blair, B. G. 1993. Russia's doomsday machine. Op. Ed. page, *The New York Times*, October 8.

Brams, S. 1994. Game theory and literature. *Games and Economic Behavior* 6 (1): 32–54.

Brokaw, A. J., and T. E. Merz. 2004. Active learning with Monty Hall in a game theory class. *Journal of Economic Education* 35 (3): 259–68.

Bulow, J., and P. Klemperer. 1999. The generalized war of attrition. *American Economic Review* 89 (1): 175–89.

Dixit, A., and B. Nalebuff. 1991. *Thinking Strategically: The Competitive Edge in Business, Politics, and Everyday Life*. New York: W. W. Norton.

Dixit, A., and S. Skeath. 2004. *Games of Strategy*, 2nd ed. New York: W. W. Norton.

Fehr, E., and S. Gächter. 2000. Cooperation and punishment in public goods experiments. *American Economic Review* 90 (4): 980–94.

Hammett, D. 1930. *The Maltese Falcon.* New York: Knopf.

Higgins, G. V. 1974. *Cogan's Trade.* New York: Knopf.

Hirshleifer, J., and J. G. Riley. 1992. *The Analytics of Uncertainty and Information.* New York: Cambridge University Press.

Nagel, R. 1995. Unraveling in guessing games: An experimental study. *American Economic Review* 85 (5): 1313–26.

Nasar, S. 1998. *A Beautiful Mind.* New York: Simon and Schuster.

Rasmusen, E., ed. 2000. *Readings in Games and Information.* Malden, MA: Blackwell Publishing.

Runyon, D. 1933. The idyll of Miss Sarah Brown. *Collier's Magazine.* Reprinted in *Guys and Dolls.* New York: Viking, 1992.

Schelling, T. C. 1960. *The Strategy of Conflict.* Cambridge: Harvard University Press.

————. 1966. *Arms and Influence.* New Haven: Yale University Press.

Simon, H. A. and J. Schaeffer. 1992. The game of chess. In R. J. Aumann and S. Hart, eds., *Handbook of Game Theory, Volume I.* Amsterdam: North-Holland.

Trandel, G. A. 1999. Using a TV game show to explain the concept of a dominant strategy. *Journal of Economic Education* 30 (2): 133–40.

Von Neumann, J., and O. Morgenstern. 1953. *Theory of Games and Economic Behavior,* 3rd ed. Princeton: Princeton University Press.

Watts, M. 2003. *The Literary Book of Economics.* Wilmington, DE: ISI Books.

Williams, J. D. 1966. *The Compleat Strategyst,* revised edition. New York: McGraw-Hill. (Reissue, New York: Dover, 1986.)

CHAPTER **2**

USING CLASSROOM EXPERIMENTS TO TEACH ECONOMICS

Denise Hazlett

A classroom experiment puts students in a controlled environment and asks them to make economic decisions. Their decisions become the data the class later analyzes. A good classroom experiment guides students through the discovery of an important economic concept, inspiring new ideas and attitudes. Experiments work best when students actively participate not only at the decision-making stage, but also in the follow-up analysis. Rather than simply accepting (or not) the instructor's presentation of theory, students formulate it themselves in their analysis of the results. Allowing students time to wrestle with their results helps them become informed critics of the applications and limitations of economic theory. As an added bonus, students typically enjoy experiments, and instructors do too. Emerson and Taylor (2004) summarized the regrettably scant literature assessing the effectiveness of classroom experiments, and reported their own finding of significant gains in student learning in classes that used experiments, compared to a control set of classes that did not.

Instructors generally do not have to start from scratch designing an experiment on the particular topic they want to cover. Since Chamberlain first ran economics experiments in his Harvard classes in the 1940s, many experiments have been developed to demonstrate a wide range of economic concepts.[1] In two sections of this chapter I describe various resources, including electronic sources, to help locate and use experiments.

I. GETTING STARTED

How can instructors know if they want to use experiments? I suggest that they look for an experiment that meshes with their teaching style, course content and goals, and give it a try. The double-auction market experiment (also called the pit market experiment) offers an excellent starting point for many undergraduate courses because it is interactive, fun, and generates a rich data set for follow-up analysis. Parker (1995) and Holt (1996) provided thorough descriptions of the experiment, so here I will give an overview.

The double auction offers a basic introduction to markets, demonstrating how prices determine production, consumption and distribution decisions in a competitive economy. The instructor assigns students the roles of potential sellers and buyers of a hypothetical good. Students begin the experiment knowing only their own cost of production or their own consumption value. They mingle, making offers to sell or offers to buy at prices they specify. As they trade and observe other trades, they begin to see how prices convey information in a decentralized economy. From an initially chaotic set of trades, the market gradually converges toward equilibrium. There are many possible extensions to the experiment, including price controls, taxes, subsidies, and other shifts in demand or supply. In one class session the instructor can typically run the basic experiment plus several extensions.

In principles of economics courses, I suggest running the double-auction market experiment before introducing the supply and demand model. In fact, many leading experimental economists recommend running experiments before introducing the theories the experiments demonstrate (Holt, 1996; Noussair and Walker, 1998; Bergstrom and Miller, 2000). If students know how theory suggests they should behave during the course of an experiment, they might conclude that this knowledge influenced their behavior during the experiment and wonder if their results would hold for people who had not studied economics. I have observed that students become more firmly convinced of the predictive power of basic economic theory if they can discover it for themselves. For example, an instructor who runs the double-auction experiment before discussing price controls will likely see buyers greet the announcement of a price ceiling with enthusiasm. But after a few minutes of thwarted attempts to trade at that price, many buyers become disillusioned with the idea of a price ceiling.

The double auction offers an excellent complement to lecture. It not only generates lecture examples, but it makes students (who have personal experience to refer to and build on) the experts in the discussion. In the debriefing, students gain a better grasp of what demand and supply curves mean, as they build these curves from the information the instructor gives them (after the experiment) about each buyer's willingness to pay and each seller's cost of production. The related concepts of consumer and producer surplus become clearer to students who have searched for those gains in the experiment. In short, abstract concepts become concrete.

The double auction can be used to introduce supply and demand analysis in a principles of microeconomics, principles of macroeconomics, or combined micro/macro principles course. Alternatively, the experiment can solve the problem of how to cover supply and demand in a macro (or micro) principles course where some students need only a review, because they have already taken micro (or macro) principles. For students who have not participated in this experiment before, it gives them a fresh perspective on the supply and demand tools they *have* seen before. Even students in more advanced courses can benefit from the insight provided by this experiment. Holt (1996, p. 199) noted that this "market trading exercise would be my clear first choice if I were limited to a single lecture in a microeconomics course at any level."

II. RUNNING AND DEBRIEFING A DOUBLE-AUCTION EXPERIMENT

Participating in an experiment generates only some of the potential learning from the exercise. The rest comes from participating in the analysis of the results. The instructor should prepare follow-up questions that ask students to draw the connections between the experimental data and economic theory. See Parker (1995) and Hazlett (1999) for discussion and homework questions for several experiments, including the double-auction market. In this section I provide an extended example of how to run and debrief a double-auction experiment using the results from the experiment I ran in my principles of economics course in the spring of 2003. I ran the experiment with several extensions on the second day of class. In the next class meeting, I gave the students the hand-out that appears in Appendix 2.A, which shows the results and provides other information the students need to analyze these results, including every seller's production cost and every buyer's consumption value. The handout also includes a set of questions that we explored as a class over the next three weeks, as we developed the supply and demand model. The exam question I wrote to follow up on the experiment appears in Appendix 2.B.

When I assigned consumption values and production costs, I deliberately chose values that would *not* make the supply and demand curves mirror images of each other. Note that equally steep supply and demand curves would yield equal amounts of consumer and producer surplus. Because students seem to expect symmetry in the gains from trade, deliberately making the curves asymmetric provides food for thought. Similarly, giving the demand and supply curves nonlinear shapes, rather than the constant slope of a textbook curve, helps students understand that not all supply and demand curves look alike. Once they have absorbed this fact, students become much better equipped to actually understand what these tools represent. The graph from my exam question in part (a) of Appendix 2.B shows an example of supply and demand curves that are not mirror images of each other. Note that the curves are step functions because the item traded is indivisible.

The consumption values and production costs I assigned in the experiment generate a competitive equilibrium price between \$21 and \$22, and an equilibrium quantity of six. The actual quantity traded matched the equilibrium prediction, and by the third period the average price had moved within the equilibrium range, although some individual prices remained outside the range. I had planned to run a fourth period replicating the conditions of the first three, to see if all prices would fall within the equilibrium range. In general, however, I do not insist that we run enough periods to produce perfect data. Students generally get the idea that repetition would complete or at least continue the movement to equilibrium, without having to spend more class time proving it. In debriefing the double-auction experiment, the instructor can cite the relevant experimental research literature to confirm that repetition generates convergence to equilibrium in the research laboratory (Davis and Holt, 1993, p. 149). [2]

In this case, however, the fourth period conditions did differ from those of the first three, because after the third period one of the sellers suggested to the others that they form a seller's union to raise the price and increase their profits. Whenever someone calls for collusion, I offer to let those wishing to collude step outside to (quietly) discuss their plans. This offer gives their collusive agreement its best shot, so when their collusion breaks down, as it typically does quickly, that failure illustrates the strength of the competitive equilibrium prediction. In their review of double-auction research experiments, Davis and Holt (1993, p. 150) found no case in which sellers managed to maintain collusion, even in the "many experiments [that] involved as few as four sellers." In my class, the collusion followed the typical breakdown trajectory. While the sellers colluded outside, the buyers decided to form their own buyer's union. Both sets of collusive agreements fell apart, with only a few students holding out in Period 4.

I had planned to use the standard technique of reassigning roles and values about half-way through the experiment (see Noussair and Walker, 1998), which helps to achieve two goals. First, at the same time the instructor can change production costs or consumption values, thereby shifting the supply or demand curve. This shift generates an example for a later discussion on the ability of the market to adjust to a new equilibrium. Second, reassigning roles and values alleviates the frustration of those students who were randomly assigned high production costs or low consumption values who cannot continue to trade as the market approaches equilibrium. The students in these roles represent the tails of the supply and demand curves, so the experiment requires their presence. In fact, their experience and comments enrich the follow-up discussion of market efficiency. However, the instructor certainly does not want these students to spend the whole experiment frustrated. Fortunately, the auction extension of introducing price controls revives the excitement of the extra-marginal traders. With a price floor in place, if high-cost sellers jump in fast enough to be among the few who can sell, they can displace some lower-cost sellers. Similarly, with a price ceiling, some fast-moving low-valued buyers can displace higher-valued buyers. These actions provide fodder for a lively discussion of the advantages and disadvantages of price ceilings.

Sometimes students suggest policies, such as price controls or subsidies, to make buying or selling possible for the extra-marginal traders. In this class, students suggested that the government fund a research and development project to lower producers' costs, so that more people could afford to buy the product. After I pointed out that land-grant universities and other basic research programs provide a real-world example of this process, I implemented their R&D cost-reduction suggestion (using a $5 decrease in every seller's production cost) because I wanted to encourage their interest in exploring alternative policies. Moreover, the shift in the supply curve from the cost reduction meant that I could illustrate a change in equilibrium without having to reassign roles and production and consumption values. I also liked the fact that our later class discussions on market efficiency could include a cost-benefit analysis in which we could determine what this government R&D project would be worth to society.

The reduction in production costs did, of course, mean that the price fell and more people could trade, just as the students suspected. Even so, not everyone could trade. I implemented a price ceiling and then a price floor over the next two periods, citing as my rationale the existence of these people who could not trade.

Implementing student suggestions, such as the R&D project or the formation of a seller's union, encourages students to keep thinking and learning throughout the experiment and debriefing period. Moreover, giving serious consideration to their suggestions explicitly acknowledges the insight they develop as participants in the experimental market. Of course, I do not implement every suggestion that they make. A student suggestion typically inspires other students to discuss its relative merits. I moderate these discussions, while letting students bring up the relevant issues. For instance, later in the semester the students in this class participated in a double-auction labor market experiment demonstrating the effects of unemployment compensation on unemployment rates and wage distributions (see Hazlett, 2004). During this experiment one student suggested implementing a minimum wage. Several other students, representing both workers and employers, objected on the grounds that fewer people would have jobs as a result. After hearing this objection, the student withdrew the suggestion. Another student proposed that the government pay for public transportation to reduce workers' costs of employment, and thereby reduce unemployment. The class approved of this proposal, and I implemented it.

III. EXPERIMENTS IN COURSES AT VARIOUS LEVELS

In lower-level field courses instructors can use one of the extensions of the double-auction market and recast it for a specific application. For instance, Gillette (1996) used a demand-shift extension when he designed an experiment for a health economics course in which a third-party payer steps into a double-auction market for health care services, offering to pay 80 percent of the negotiated purchase price. Similarly, instructors of lower-level field courses might use fairly straight-forward variations of the double-auction experiment, such as Parker's (1995) product quality experiment, which illustrates how competitive markets satisfy buyers' willingness to pay for higher quality despite the extra cost to sellers. Laury and Holt (1998) provided another variation with their multi-market experiment, to illustrate how the law of one price holds across different markets.

Instructors of intermediate theory or upper-level field courses can use more complicated variations of the double-auction market experiment. For example, Hazlett (2000) described a positive externality experiment that demonstrates how buyers and sellers of education ignore spill-over benefits to third parties, thereby producing an inefficiently low level of education. In a public finance course, the experiment can help to introduce the economic rationale for government provision (or government subsidies) of goods and services that generate positive externalities, such as education. This experiment also explores the ability of private negotiations to internalize a positive externality in a competitive market. When the instructor encourages the recipients of the spill-over benefits to consider how they might act to make themselves better off, they typically offer to subsidize education, thereby maximizing their own net benefits. In the debriefing, the class discusses whether such privately offered scholarships, which generate the socially optimal quantity of education under the controlled conditions of the classroom laboratory, could overcome the free-rider problem in the real world. A similar experiment (Crouter, 2003) has fly-fishers receiving spill-over benefits from the water left in rivers when hydroelectric companies purchase irrigation rights from farmers. In the competitive equilibrium, farmers sell too few water rights to the hydroelectric companies, because both parties ignore the spill-over benefits to the fly-fishers. When the instructor encourages the fly-fishers to act in their own interest, they offer to subsidize the sale of water rights, thereby moving the equilibrium to the social optimum.

Several double-auction experiments exist to demonstrate the advantages of marketable pollution permits in environmental economics courses. Hazlett and Bakkensen (forthcoming) describe a fairly complex version in which students represent electrical utility companies that trade carbon dioxide permits. This experiment emphasizes the difference between permit trading at the national and international levels, and explores the effects of such trading on a developed and a developing country.

In a macroeconomic theory course, a double-auction federal funds market experiment (Hazlett, 2003) demonstrates how the Federal Open Market Committee (FOMC) influences the federal funds rate. Most of the students in this experiment take the roles of banks, which borrow or lend in a market for overnight bank loans. The remaining students operate the Federal Reserve Open Market Trading Desk. The instructor takes the role of the FOMC, issuing directives that specify interest rate targets. The students operating the trading desk must decide what quantity of open market sales or purchases to make, based on the latest FOMC directive. The open market operations change the quantity of excess reserves in the banks, thereby changing the equilibrium interest rate in the federal funds market. The experiment helps students understand why an open market sale or purchase changes the federal funds rate, and in what direction.

In a money and banking or monetary theory course, a double-auction credit market experiment (Hazlett, 2005) demonstrates how inflation variability causes a wealth transfer between borrowers and lenders. More important, this experiment shows the social cost that results when lenders and borrowers cannot agree on a nominal interest rate that compensates each for the risk caused by inflation variability. The social cost of inflation uncertainty shows up here as a failure of the credit market to allocate funds to the highest-valued investment projects.

In addition to the double auction variations that lend themselves to field courses, there are many other experiments that do not rely on the double-auction market institution at all. In fact, so many classroom experiments now exist in a range of fields and levels that instructors will likely find one that demonstrates the particular point they want to make. Sources for these experiments follow the next section.

IV. COMPUTERIZED VERSUS HAND-RUN EXPERIMENTS

An instructor who decides to use a classroom experiment must choose whether to run it by hand or using computers. In a hand-run experiment, the instructor typically distributes written instructions and private information slips establishing each student's role. These hand-run experiments generally take place during class time, in the classroom, with students interacting face-to-face. By contrast, a computerized experiment has each student (or sometimes small teams of students) sitting at a computer. This kind of experiment can take place during class time, with the entire class in a computer laboratory, or with each student logged onto a networked computer either on or even off campus. More commonly, however, computerized experiments take place outside of the regular class time. In some computerized experiments, all students log on and interact simultaneously, that is, in a synchronous manner. In others, students log on at their convenience and make their decisions asynchronously.

On the question of whether to run experiments by hand or by computer, I suggest that instructors use whichever method they find most comfortable, as long as all the students are able to participate. Especially in large classes, it is more exciting and meaningful to participate than to watch a subsection of the class conduct the experiment. Professors have successfully run experiments by hand in classes as large as 75 to 100.[3] The time spent recording trades makes the double-auction experiment difficult to run by hand in very large classes, but a student assistant helping to record trades can reduce this time considerably. I do not recommend asking a student from the class itself to fulfill this role, if it prevents the student from participating in the experiment. Actual participation provides too much insight (and too much fun) to give it up lightly.

Fortunately, there is a new set of resources to help overcome the double-auction data-recording burden. Murphy (2004) provided a Windows-based program for the instructor to record trades and project them on a screen where all can see. The program works with any number of buyers and sellers, and with whatever production costs and consumption values the instructor chooses. Murphy's program saves the data in a simple text file, from which the instructor can use an Excel spreadsheet to plot the supply and demand graphs and the trades. An instructor recording trades on a blackboard rather than a computer can still use Murphy's spreadsheet to create the graphs and display the results.

When uncertain about choosing between hand-run or computerized experiments, instructors could consider using both. For instance, an initial double-auction market experiment run by hand gives students face-to-face experience and allows the instructor the flexibility to implement student suggestions. Computerized experiments could cover topics later in the term.

V. SOURCES OF INFORMATION ON COMPUTERIZED EXPERIMENTS

Holt (2004a) provided free access to over 30 of his web-based programs for running experiments. In addition, Holt's (2004b) book *Markets, Games and Strategic Behavior: Recipes for Interactive Learning* described how to use these computerized experiments in the classroom. The Economic Science Laboratory at the University of Arizona offers free access to several experiments an instructor can run online via EconPort, at <http://www.econport.org:8080/econport/request?page=web_home>.

The educational technology company Aplia <http://content.aplia.com/downloads/ApliaExperimentGuide.pdf> offers a set of web-based synchronous experiments as a component of its commercial course management system.[4] These experiments are run on Aplia's server, with students and the instructor interacting via browser-enabled computers. Each experiment includes a complete set of interactive teaching resources: instructions, a computer-graded quiz on the instructions, participation in the experiment itself and a display of results, a follow-up reading that guides students through an analysis of the experiment, and a set of computer-graded questions to check each student's understanding of the analysis. The *Aplia Experiment Guide*, an online pdf document, provides a fast introduction to Aplia's double-auction experiment. Instructors can see all of Aplia's materials and participate in demonstrations of the experiments free of charge.

VI. SOURCES OF INFORMATION ON HAND-RUN EXPERIMENTS

Delemeester and Brauer (2004) maintain and annually update a searchable online index: Games That Economists Play: Non-Computerized Classroom Games for

College Economics. Their site indexes working papers, journal publications, and their online newsletter *Classroom Expernomics*. Bergstrom and Miller (2000) wrote an entire principles of microeconomics textbook built around classroom experiments. In addition, several textbook publishers offer instructor's manuals on experiments as free supplements to their texts (Ortmann and Colander, 1995; Delemeester and Neral 1995; Hazlett, 1999; Yandell, 2002). Parker (1993) wrote one of the first manuals on how to use classroom experiments. His (1995) Using Laboratory Experiments to Teach Introductory Economics remains a classic for its depth of coverage.

The National Science Foundation has funded a Teaching Innovations Program to provide college and university economics instructors with hands-on help to learn how to use interactive teaching techniques, including experiments. The program runs from 2005 to 2009 and includes a three-day summer workshop, plus a web-based follow-on component to help participants plan how to introduce interactive teaching into their own courses. For more information on this program, visit the website of the sponsor, the American Economic Association's Committee on Economic Education: <www.vanderbilt.edu/AEA/AEACEE>.

VII. GENERAL SUGGESTIONS ON RUNNING EXPERIMENTS

When running any experiment, instructors should keep several points in mind. First and foremost, students must understand the instructions, or they will feel frustrated and make random decisions that muddy the results. At the beginning of a hand-run experiment, I distribute written instructions and read them aloud, pausing for questions. With computerized experiments run outside of class, it generally works well to have students read the instructions online, where they typically become familiar with the experimental interface.

Instructors should consider how to motivate students to arrive on time for experiments and follow instructions. To this end, I base a small portion of the course grade on attentive participation. Despite the instructor's best efforts to motivate students to arrive on time, some will come late to class. When late arrivals have missed enough of the instructions to make them unable to participate on their own, I pair them with a student who arrived on time.

Many of the experiments I use require students to maximize hypothetical earnings. Students generally respond to this challenge because they find the experiments interesting. To maintain that interest and ensure a good learning experience, the instructor should choose experiments that promote deeper understanding of an important concept than students could get from a brief explanation, or that they would not remember without a concrete example. The exercise should have students making decisions that hold their attention, without being so complex that they become frustrated.

Some experiments, such as prisoner dilemma games or voluntary contribution mechanisms, do not work as well with hypothetical earnings (see Noussair and Walker, 1998). In these cases, I pay off with chocolate proportional to the student's earnings. Some instructors award extra credit points in a similar manner, for a wide range of experiments. However, in some experiments many students will have higher earnings than others simply because they start in more favorable positions. For instance, in a double-auction experiment, a seller with a low cost of production has greater potential earnings than a seller with a high cost. Over the course of several experiments, this random component to earnings tends to average out. An instructor who issues grades (or other goodies) based on the earnings from multiple class experiments might rely on that averaging-out effect. However, instructors should keep in mind that combining a grade for the experimental outcome with a curved course grade could change the experiment from an exercise in profit maximization into a zero-sum game.

When experiments are under way, instructors should watch for and help confused students, but refrain from actually telling students what actions to take. In particular, instructors should never announce what they expect to happen during the experiment, or intervene to affect the outcome. If they do, students might simply do what the instructor wants, and then the exercise loses its teaching value. For example, if students feel that a double-auction market converged because the instructor suggested that buyers pay more and sellers charge less, then they will not recognize the power of markets to find the equilibrium price without intervention.

The cardinal rule of research experiments also applies to classroom experiments. Never lie to the participants. For example, an instructor who tells students that they will receive earnings according to the choices they make in a prisoner's dilemma game must distribute the earnings as promised, and not give in to the temptation to smooth ruffled feathers by rewarding everyone equally. The instructor must maintain credibility over the entire course, otherwise students will not believe the instructions in future experiments, and might instead behave in a manner that looks random, rather than illustrating the point the instructor wants to make.

Finally, the debriefing sessions should give students the opportunity to analyze the experimental data. A fast explanation from the instructor may seem like an efficient way to impart knowledge, but it cannot adequately replace the benefits students get from their own attempts to interpret the results.

VIII.   DO'S AND DON'TS

- Do choose experiments that promote deep understanding.
- Do motivate participants to behave as they would in a true market situation, in order to make the experience and results useful.
- Don't use a lengthy experiment to demonstrate a concept that students could easily master from a brief explanation.

- Do choose experiments consistent with your course goals and your teaching style.
- Do choose experiments that provide opportunities for students to make decisions, so that the activity holds their interest.
- Do choose experiments that allow every student to participate.
- Do consider carefully how much of the relevant economic theory students will need to know in advance, versus what they can discover from participating and analyzing their results.
- Do motivate students to arrive on time, but don't rely on everyone arriving on time.
- Do consider arranging for an assistant to help distribute instructions and record results, especially in large classes.
- Do distribute a copy of the instructions for hand-run experiments to each student, read them aloud, and pause for student questions.
- Don't tell participants what you expect to happen during the experiment, or step in to influence the outcome.
- Do watch for confused students and offer them more help to understand the instructions.
- Do consider implementing on-the-spot the suggestions that students make during the experiment.
- Don't lie to or mislead the participants.
- Don't insist that a double-auction experiment continue enough periods to produce perfect data once it is clear that the market has nearly converged to equilibrium.
- Do prepare follow-up questions that encourage students to analyze the results, either as a writing assignment or an in-class discussion.
- Don't circumvent the learning process by providing the follow-up analysis yourself, before students have had a chance to wrestle with the results.
- Don't turn the experiment into a zero-sum game by combining a grade for the experimental outcome with a curved course grade.
- Do put questions on course exams that cover what students have learned from the experiments.

APPENDIX 2.A: Double-Auction Experiment Debriefing Hand-Out[5]

You have participated in an experiment using a double-auction market. Below are the values given to each buyer and seller in the experiment, as well as the experimental results. When we do experiments in the future, I will ask you to write a report in essay form using economic theory to interpret the experimental results. For example, a lab report on the double-auction experiment you performed would address the discussion questions below. For this first experiment, we will answer these questions together in class. Please bring this hand-out to class with you for the next three weeks.

Experiment Data Values for Buyers and Sellers

Buyer's ID number	Buyer's consumption value ($)	Seller's ID letter	Seller's cost of production ($)
1	20	A	25
2	26	B	23
3	21	C	22
4	23	D	21
5	23	E	20
6	24	F	19
7	21	G	16
8	26	H	15
9	27	J	15
10	19	K	27
11	19	L	27
12	18	M	26

Results

Period 1   8H 23 (i.e., Buyer 8 bought a widget from Seller H at a price of $23) 2F 22, 3G 21, 5D 23, 9C 24, 4J 21

Period 2   5E 22, 4D 22, 1A 26, 2C 23, 9F 23, 8H 21

Period 3   2B 23, 5E 22, 4C 23, 8F 22, 9D 22, 5H 19

Before Period 4 began, the sellers attempted to establish a sellers' union. In response, the buyers attempted to establish a buyers' union. The members of these unions dissolved their unions before Period 4 trading began.

Period 4   8H 21, 4C 23, 2B 24, 5F 21, 4D 22

Before Period 5 began, the government funded a research and development project. This project generated a technology that lowered all producers' costs by $5. The costs of production remained low in Periods 6 and 7.

Period 5   7F 19, 4D 20, 5B 19, 9H 20, 8E 20, 2C 19.5, 3G 19, 10J 19

Price ceiling: In period 6, no one could legally sell a widget for more than $17.50.

Period 6   3C 17.5, 2F 17.5, 4G 17.5, 9H 16.5, 11D 17.5, 5E 16, 8J 16.5

Price floor: In period 7, no one could legally sell a widget for less than $23.

Period 7   54K 23, 8J 23, 5B 23, 2M 23, 9H 23

Questions

1. Consider Periods 1 through 4, the periods before the government conducted its research and development project. Graph the demand curve for widgets. (Hint: You find the demand curve from buyers' given values, not from the results of

the experiment.) Graph the supply curve for widgets. (Hint: you find the supply curve from sellers' costs, not from the results of the experiment.) What price and quantity does economic theory predict will prevail in equilibrium? How would you measure potential gains from trade in the market? (Hint: these gains are referred to as consumer and producer surplus.) Now consider the actual trades in Periods 1 through 4. Was the outcome in terms of quantity exchanged, price, and gains from trade what you would expect based on theory?

2. Consider Period 5, in which sellers' costs of production all fell by $5. What now are the market demand and supply curves? (Again, this is a question about the buyers' values and sellers' costs, not a question about the results.) What price and quantity does theory predict now? What are the potential gains from trade? How much of these potential gains are caused by the government's project to improve technology? How much do you think we as taxpayers should be willing to pay to have the government conduct such a project? Finally, how do the actual results in Period 5 (price, quantity, gains) compare to those predicted by theory?

3. What does economic theory predict would happen in Period 6, with a price ceiling of $17.50? What does theory predict would happen in Period 7, with a price floor of $23? Were the results in Period 6 and 7 what you would expect based on theory?

4.   How closely did the experimental market compare to the textbook paradigm of a competitive market, both in terms of assumptions, and in terms of the actual prices and quantity exchanged? What were the principal similarities and differences?

APPENDIX 2.B: Exam Question with Sample Answers

Note: I distributed the following exam question to test concepts students learned from the double-auction experiment with price controls. One student's answers appear in *italics* and brackets. To create the graph to answer part (a), I used the Excel spreadsheet found in Murphy (2004).

Question

Suppose a market for widgets is perfectly competitive and free of government intervention. Sellers' costs of production and buyers' consumption values are given below, in dollars. Each buyer may buy at most one widget and each seller may sell at most one widget. No fractional units of widgets can be traded. Prices can be negotiated to the penny. Use the data below to answer the following questions.

Buyer and Seller Values

Buyer's ID number	Buyer's consumption value ($)	Seller's ID letter	Seller's cost of production ($)
1	5	A	5
2	9	B	2
3	12	C	10
4	13	D	4
5	14	E	10
6	14	F	12
7	11	G	14
8	5	H	7
9	8	J	6
10	6	K	4

(a) On the attached graph paper, draw the supply and demand graph for widgets. Be sure to label your axes.

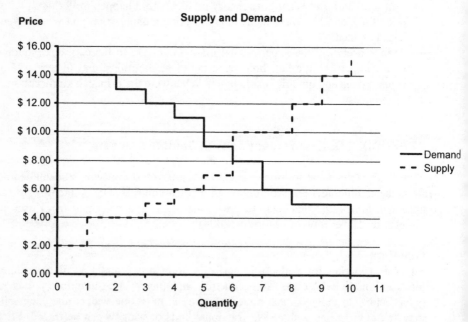

(b) What is the equilibrium price range for widgets? Recall that prices can be negotiated to the penny. *[$8.00 to $9.00]*

(c) What is the equilibrium quantity of widgets? *[6]*

(d) What is the total consumer surplus in equilibrium?

[total value = (2)$14 + $13 + $12 + $11 + $9 = $73
total paid = $9 × 6 = $54
total consumer surplus = $73 – $54 = $19]
(e) What is the total producer surplus in equilibrium?
[total revenue = $9 × 6 = $54
total cost = $2 + (2)$4 + $5 + $6 + $7 = $28
total producer surplus = $54 – $28 = $26]

Suppose that in order to help producers, the government sets a price floor of $11.50. With the price floor in place, the trades described in the following table occur.

Trades with a Price Floor in Place

Seller's ID number	Buyer's ID number	Price ($)	Seller's producer surplus	Buyer's consumer surplus
C	5	11.50	*[$1.50]*	*[$2.50]*
H	6	11.50	*[$4.50]*	*[$2.50]*
K	4	11.50	*[$7.50]*	*[$1.50]*
J	3	11.50	*[$5.50]*	*[$0.50]*

(f) Fill in the table above to show the actual producer surplus and consumer surplus associated with each trade.
(g) Would you say that the price floor helped producers? Explain.
[The price floor was detrimental to the success of producers. Although the producers who were able to sell widgets were able to make a profit, many producers were not able to sell, for as the price of the good increased beyond equilibrium price, the quantity of the good demanded decreased. Therefore, the total producer surplus decreased from $26.00 to $19.00. The price floor did not help producers overall.]
(h) How was society in general affected by the price floor?
[Society in general was hurt by the price floor. Just as fewer producers were able to enter the market, fewer buyers were able to enter the market, as well. Total consumer surplus decreased form $19.00 to $7.00. Moreover, total gains from trade (PS + CS) decreased from $45.00 to $26.00. The price floor was detrimental to society overall.]

NOTES

[1] Bergstrom and Kwok (2005) described Edward Chamberlain's early experimentation in the classroom, and also that of Vernon Smith. They noted that Chamberlain used experiments to demonstrate that prices do not tend towards the competitive equilibrium prediction, whereas Smith used experiments to demonstrate the opposite. Bergstrom

and Kwok described the differences between Chamberlain and Smith's experimental designs, and then analyzed the results of a classroom experiment with an intermediate design. They found that as traders became more familiar with market conditions, they behaved more in keeping with predictions from competitive theory and less like profit-splitters.

[2] A research experiment allows the researcher to test economic theory under controlled conditions, whereas a classroom experiment gives participants a better understanding of theory. For more information about research experiments, see Davis and Holt (1993), Friedman and Sunder (1994), and Kagel and Roth (1995).

[3] Cynthia Hill of Idaho State University runs the double auction by hand in her principles of macroeconomics course with 80 students, as does Michael Haupert of the University of Wisconsin – La Crosse in his principles of economics course with 100 students. Arlington Williams of Indiana University has used the hand-run double auction in sections up to 75. For larger classes, he runs out-of-class computerized experiments so that everyone can participate.

[4] Aplia <aplia.com> grew from Paul Romer's commitment to design experiments for his intermediate macroeconomics students at Stanford University.

[5] This handout is similar to handouts Jeffrey Parker gives his Reed College students.

REFERENCES

Aplia Experiment Guide online at: <http://content.aplia.com/downloads/ApliaExperiment Guide.pdf>.

Bergstrom, T., and E. Kwok. 2005. Extracting valuable data from classroom trading pits. *Journal of Economic Education* 36 (Summer).

Bergstrom, T., and J. Miller. 2000. *Experiments with Economic Principles*. 2nd ed. Boston: Irwin McGraw-Hill.

Crouter, J. 2003. A water bank game with fishy externalities. *Review of Agricultural Economics* 25 (1): 246–58.

Davis, D., and C. Holt. 1993. *Experimental Economics*. Princeton: Princeton University Press.

Delemeester, G., and J. Brauer. 2004. Games that economists play: Non-computerized classroom games for college economics. An online index at: <http://www.marietta.edu/~delemeeg/games/>.

Delemeester, G., and J. Neral. 1995. *Classroom Experiments: A User's Guide*. Boston: Houghton-Mifflin.

———. eds. *Classroom Expernomics*. An electronic journal online at: <http://mcnet.marietta.edu/~delemeeg/expernom.html>. Accessed January 4, 2005.

Emerson, T., and B. Taylor. 2004. Comparing student achievement across experimental and lecture-oriented sections of a principles of microeconomics course. *Southern Economic Journal* 70 (3): 672–93.

Friedman, D., and S. Sunder. 1994. *Experimental Methods: A Primer for Economists*. Cambridge: Cambridge University Press.

Gillette, D. 1996. Double-oral auctions and health care. Working paper, Truman State University.

Hazlett, D. 1999. *Economic Experiments in the Classroom.* Reading, MA: Addison Wesley.

———. 2000. An experimental education market with positive externalities. *Journal of Economic Education* 31 (1): 44–51.

———. 2003. A classroom federal funds rate experiment. Whitman College working paper. Online at: <http://people.whitman.edu/~hazlett/econ>.

———. 2004. A classroom unemployment compensation experiment. *Southern Economic Journal* (70) 3: 694–704.

———. 2005. A classroom inflation uncertainty experiment. Whitman College working paper.

Hazlett, D., and L. Bakkensen. Forthcoming. Global trade in CO_2 permits: A classroom experiment. *Perspectives on Economic Education Research.*

Holt, C. 1996. Classroom games: Trading in a pit market. *Journal of Economic Perspectives* 10 (1): 193–203.

———. 2004a. Computer programs for classroom games. Online at <http://www.people.virginia.edu/~cah2k/programs.html>.

———. 2004b. *Markets, Games and Strategic Behavior: Recipes for Interactive Learning.* Online at <http://www.people.Virginia.EDU/~cah2k/expbooknsf.pdf>.

Kagel, J., and A. Roth. 1995. *The Handbook of Experimental Economics.* Princeton: Princeton University Press.

Laury, S., and C. Holt. 1999. Multi-market equilibrium, trade, and the law of one price. *Southern Economic Journal* 65 (3): 611–21.

Murphy, J. J. 2004. A simple program to conduct a hand-run double auction in the classroom. *Journal of Economic Education* 35 (2): 212. Available online at <http://www.umass.edu/resec/faculty/murphy/handda/handda.html#parameters>.

Noussair, C., and J. Walker. 1998. Student decision making as active learning: Experimental economics in the classroom. In W. E. Becker and M. Watts, eds., *Teaching Economics to Undergraduates: Alternatives to Chalk and Talk.* Northampton, MA: Edward Elgar.

Ortmann, A., and D. Colander. 1995. *Experiments in Teaching and in Understanding Economics.* Chicago: Irwin.

Parker, J. 1993. Economics 210 Instructor's Laboratory Manual. Reed College working manuscript.

———. 1995. Using Laboratory Experiments to Teach Introductory Economics. Reed College working manuscript. Available at: <http://academic.reed.edu/economics/faculty/parker/exp.html>.

Yandell, D. 2002. *Using Experiments, Cases, and Activities in the Classroom,* 2nd ed. Upper Saddle River, NJ: Prentice Hall.

CHAPTER **3**

THE EVOLUTION OF COOPERATIVE LEARNING AND ECONOMICS INSTRUCTION

Robin L. Bartlett

Cooperative learning is still relatively new, but it is evolving rapidly. Elementary and secondary school teachers began incorporating cooperative learning into their classes in the late 1980s, including economics lessons in grades K-12. (See National Council on Economic Education's website <www.ncee.net> for examples). At the undergraduate level, Maier and Keenan (1994) and Keenan and Maier (1994) developed some of the first cooperative learning exercises in economics and continue to do so (Maier, 2001). Moore (1998) developed an out-of-class collaborative learning lab (CLL) for his introductory microeconomics students, who indicated on a survey that they enjoyed the experience and felt that they had benefited from the labs. Khandker and Elfessi (2000) built on Moore's idea of an out-of-class CLL and were able to document its effectiveness in improving scores on standardized tests compared to scores for students who had not used it. Brooks and Khandker (2002) brought Moore's out-of-class CLL into their classroom, and found that in small classes, but not in large classes, the CLL experience significantly improved student performance on final exams. These studies show that cooperative learning is becoming a viable alternative to the "chalk and talk" commonly used in undergraduate economics courses (Becker and Watts, 2001a; 2001b; 1998; 1996; 1995).

I. THE PIONEERS OF COOPERATIVE LEARNING

Johnson and Johnson (1999; 1989), along with collaborators (Johnson, Johnson, and Holubec, 1993; Johnson, Johnson, and Smith, 1991a), pioneered the concept of cooperative learning. The purpose of a cooperative group is to ensure that individuals within a group take responsibility for their own learning as well as that of other students in their group. Research reviewed by Bruffee (1993), Johnson, Johnson, and Smith (1991b), Kagan (1994), Sharan (1990), and Slavin (1990; 1999) on the effects of cooperative learning environments suggests that they offer better learning environments: Students learn more and learn more effectively, become more involved in the subject matter, and have lower attrition rates.

Astin (1993) and Qin, Johnson, and Johnson (1995) have conducted two major studies on educational environments and student performance. Astin, whose sample included over 27,000 students at more than 300 institutions, found that the two most important variables for student academic success and satisfaction were positive student-to-student interactions and positive student-to-instructor interactions. Both of these variables were more important than either curriculum (arts, humanities, sciences, or social sciences) or content (disciplines within curriculum) variables. Student-to-student interactions are the benchmark of cooperative learning activities and positive student-to-faculty interactions were the key to their success.

Qin, Johnson, and Johnson (1995) performed a meta-analysis of cooperative learning studies that compared performances of students in cooperative learning environments with those of students in competitive learning environments. They found that the cooperative learning group developed stronger problem-solving skills. We now also know that cooperative learning works not only for students in grades K-12, but also for undergraduates. Nilson (2003) reviewed the studies that show students in cooperative learning environments improve learning of content, develop interpersonal skills, and increase self-esteem.

There is some evidence to suggest that cooperative learning techniques help mitigate stereotypes (Cabrera, Crissman, Bernal, Nora, Terenzini, and Pascarella, 2002; Ginorio, 1995; Ingram and Parker, 2002; Miller and Harrington, 1990; Slavin, 1990, Chapter 4). Mathematics instructors have found that cooperative learning techniques increased the performance of women (Adedayo, 1998; Committee on Undergraduate Science Education, 1997) and students of color. Treisman (1992) showed that cooperative learning techniques improved the performance of African American students in calculus at the University of California at Berkeley. Duncan and Dick (2000) at the University of Oregon confirmed Treisman's findings. Students of color performed better in introductory mathematics courses in cooperative learning environments. Vaughan (2002) found that cooperative learning positively affects the attitudes of students of color. Potthast (1999) taught four statistics topics to one class using cooperative learning techniques and taught the same topics to another class using traditional lectures. The cooperative learning group did better on two of the four topics and the same on the remaining two topics. Blignaut and Venter (1998) from the University of Western Cape in South Africa used a test to create student teams in their statistics and computer science courses. The test results indicated which roles each student should play to ensure a balance of abilities, skill levels, and learning styles on each team. Students in teams scored higher on standardized exams than students working alone. Cox and Junkin (2002) found that the scores of students who were taught introductory physics with cooperative learning groups rather than traditional lectures/laboratory work improved on standardized tests by 50 to 100 percent.

In the social sciences, Zimbardo, Butler, and Wolfe (2003) found that in introductory psychology classes where students were allowed to take exams collaboratively with another student, average test scores were higher and the overall variance was lower. Nordstom (1996) and McCarthy and Anderson (2000) found cooperative learning techniques more effective than traditional techniques in teaching environmental management and political science courses, respectively.

Cooperative learning techniques are being used in a variety of economics courses. Schmidt (2003) demonstrated how the World Wide Web could be used with cooperative learning groups to simulate historical economic events and to illustrate public finance and economic growth principles. Cohn (1999) found that cooperative learning groups improved student performance in introductory macroeconomics classes. Johnston, James, Lye, and McDonald (2000) at the University of Melbourne also found cooperative learning techniques useful. They compared the performance of over 300 students in an experimental group to that of randomly selected students in a comparably sized control group in intermediate macroeconomics and found similar significant improvements of the former group's performance on standardized tests. White (1997) used teams to teach the economics of public policy analyses. As predicted, students who were on teams outperformed other students. Many of the instructional techniques used by experimental economists are inherently collaborative as students buy and sell resources with each other to simulate a market.

II. COOPERATIVE LEARNING GROUPS

Economics instructors frequently assign students to work in groups for class presentations, papers, or other projects. Yet groups are not necessarily cooperative learning groups, and do not always operate as effectively and efficiently as most economics instructors would like. Students may gather for study or work sessions and find that one student has done all the preparation and ends up teaching the material to other, less-prepared students. Whereas the one student who is teaching is actively engaged in learning, the other students who are listening and taking in the material are passively learning.

Putting students in undefined groups to accomplish an educational task is like putting five relatively talented students on a basketball court and directing them to score as many points as possible by throwing the basketball through the hoop at the designated end of the court. Unless each student is assigned a role to play within an overall game plan, the group will not perform very efficiently or up to its potential.

There are three basic types of cooperative groups: informal, formal, and base groups (Johnson et al., 1991b). Informal groups can be spontaneous groupings for an in-depth discussion of an economic concept or principle that has just been presented by the instructor to the class. Formal groups occur when students are assigned to groups for larger assignments such as papers and presentations that take a significant amount of time to develop. Base groups consist of students who stay together to accomplish or to complete a variety of tasks for the duration of a course. Base groups have been getting increasing attention in the undergraduate (Giordano and Hammer, 1999; Hansen and Stephens, 2000; Stein and Hurd, 2000; Yuan and Benson, 2000) and business education literatures (Manzer and Bialik, 1997; Miglietti, 2002; Vik, 2001). Base groups differ in the degree to which they are structured. Collaborative base groups are the least structured and are found most often in the sciences. Team base groups are the most structured and are found most often in business programs at the undergraduate and master of business levels.

Elements for Success

Any cooperative learning activity must have five key elements in place and functioning well for it to be successful (Meyers and Jones, 1993). The first key element is positive interdependence. This means that each student's success depends upon the support of the other students in the group. Support can be tangible as well as intangible. Tangible support may come in the form of sharing critical information, a new perspective, or acquired skill. Intangible support may come in the form of encouragement, patience, and respect. The type of support that students need may vary. Support from the instructor comes in designing and monitoring cooperative learning activities. Each goal of a cooperative learning exercise must be carefully thought through and the activities should be designed to achieve the learning objective. Economics instructors move from being a "sage on the stage" to a "guide on the side." Much like an Outward Bound instructor, economics instructors can suggest to students the kinds of equipment and resources that they will need to have in their backpacks to make the journey, and can even help them learn how to read a map. But when it comes time for them to start the journey, the instructor gives them a map and sends them on their way. Whether, when and how they make it to their destination depends on everyone in the group. The guide is there to help when they get lost.

The second key element of cooperative learning activity is face-to-face interaction between students. Students need time in class to engage in conversations with members of their groups. Talking about economics helps students learn the language of economics and gives them quick and helpful feedback on how well they understand a concept. Unfortunately, because of the logistics of getting students together on most urban campuses and the tendency for students to be over-involved on residential campuses, the chance of productive group interactions occurring outside of regular class time is minimal. Nonetheless, instructors do not have to relinquish that much of their class time to cooperative learning exercises, just enough time for the groups to carry out specific tasks. Allowing students time to get to know each other and to work through group processing and logistics problems saves the instructor and the students time in the long run. Once groups are formed and functioning, Nilson (2003, p. 134) uses the "rule of three before me." If students have questions on the material, they must ask at least three other students the question before asking the instructor. Any confusion that remains may be a management issue; that is, the instructor may not have given students adequate information or instruction on the goal of the exercise. Or, the confusion may be a preparation issue; that is, students may not have done their reading and homework. It is helpful to clarify what type of issue is present.

The third key element stressed in recent literature on cooperative learning activities is the size and composition of the groups. The consensus is that groups can be as small as two and as large as seven depending upon the cooperative learning activity. Smaller groups are good for informal and spontaneous exercises; larger groups are better for discussions of topics with no right or wrong answers. For base groups and teams, three to four students per group is the most workable number.

The composition of groups is a little trickier. The literature suggests that an equal distribution of men and women is desirable, but in economics there may be one female to every three males in upper-level courses. Even introductory courses are often less than 50 percent female. The number of minority students in economics classes is even smaller. Thus, there is little an instructor can do to prevent gender dynamics from surfacing in mixed-sex groups or racial stereotyping in classes with only a few students of color. A random assignment to groups does not seem to exacerbate these situations and many students tend to prefer luck rather than some attributed characteristic or identified difference as a basis for determining group membership. Students should only select their own groups when informal groups are being used and the students happen to be sitting next to each other. The role of the instructor with regard to this composition element is to help students develop group identity. Ice-breaking exercises (Scearce, 1992; Williams, 1993) on the first day of group assignment are great for accomplishing this, as is having students come up with a group name.

The fourth element of cooperative learning activities is accountability. Individual students need to be accountable for their actions and performance and the group must be accountable as well. Assigning roles is one way to help keep every member on a team focused and on task. These roles have to be defined, agreed upon, and evaluated. The roles that frequently appear in the literature are recorder, facilitator, encourager, summarizer, runner, elaborator, checker, and accuracy coach. The recorder writes down the group's discussion; the facilitator makes sure that everyone is heard and has space to speak; the encourager prompts students to clarify or elaborate on a point; the accuracy coach makes sure definitions and relationships are consistent with material in the book or lectures; the summarizer pulls together what the group is saying; the checker makes sure the group has done what it was supposed to do; and the runner makes sure the group's result or results get to the appropriate place. Depending upon the size of the group, students may have to play more than one role. Students then evaluate how well each student performed their roles.

In addition, instructors must find ways to monitor the group process and individual contributions. The idea of additional paperwork or evaluation procedures may seem daunting at first, but they can be easily done. For informal groups no monitoring or evaluation is needed as long as students are making reasonable arguments and coming up with useful insights during classroom activities. Formal groups do not need to be monitored, but the contributions of individual students to their projects do need to be evaluated. An evaluation sheet (Figure 3.1) can be distributed to each member of a group for completion, or made part of the course management system.

Team Member Peer Evaluation

Team Name / Number: _____

In the space provided below, please list the names of your team members – including yourself – and circle the number that best describes each team member's contribution to the team project, using the following scale (10 is high). You may also comment on each team member's contribution.

Team Member	Rating	Comments
1.	0 2 4 6 8 10	
2.	0 2 4 6 8 10	
3.	0 2 4 6 8 10	
4.	0 2 4 6 8 10	

Figure 3.1: Sample peer assessment instrument.

Students are asked to use a scale of 0 to 10 like the one shown in Figure 3.1 or a scale of 1 to 4 to rate their colleagues in terms of quantity and quality of their contributions to the project. The instructor should provide a sample set of descriptions of what each number represents, or preferably, the instructor should lead a short discussion allowing students to define what each number signifies. The discussion serves two purposes. First, students take ownership of the process. Second, and more important, each student has the same understanding of what the numbers mean.

For base groups with on-going projects such as term papers, the activities and interactions of group members need to be monitored more frequently so that intervention, if needed, takes place soon enough to help the group work effectively. For example, instructors may want to walk students through the various stages of writing a research paper and have students turn in components of their paper along the way. After each component is turned in, students can be asked to evaluate their contribution and that of their teammates to that particular component of the project. Students who under-perform during the early stages of the process then receive feedback and have an opportunity to improve their contributions to the group. After instructors review the individual team assessment instruments, they then give oral or written feedback to each team and to individual members. Early, specific feedback minimizes the future inter-ventions.

Besides developing and monitoring group-meeting skills, the instructor's role in accountability also includes determining how the cooperative learning exercises will be weighted in each student's final grade. There is general agreement in the literature on cooperative learning that relative grading schemes, such as grading on the curve, are a bad idea for cooperative learning environments because they bring competition back into the classroom. Absolute grading schemes are better because they give the group a specific goal, a level of achievement to attain. Of course goals must be not only well defined, but also achievable. The percentage of grades distributed to groups or to their members in each grade category is not predetermined. If every team performs at an exceptional level then everyone in the class receives an A. It is recommended that the weight given to cooperative learning exercises should be between 20 and 60 percent. The cooperative learning component must count enough so that students work hard, but not so much that students feel their grade is totally out of their own individual control.

The fifth element of success for cooperative learning groups is development of social skills. Students who are more reticent in class, who feel isolated or different, or who have learning disabilities, can more easily find their voice in smaller groups. Being able to talk economics with other students improves the learning process by giving these students an opportunity to gain confidence in expressing their ideas. Traditional students will also be exposed to a more diverse population of students, a population similar to that which they will likely work in after graduation. In particular, students will learn how to listen, how to respect the strengths and weaknesses of other students, and how to resolve conflicts with other students.

Basic Cooperative Learning Activities

For instructors who want to begin using cooperative learning methods, there are a number of basic activities, or game plans, and several variations on each activity that can be used depending upon the goals of the instructor.

- *Think-Pair-and-Share* is an exercise where students turn to a student on either side of them and discuss an issue. These exercises are used to develop and reinforce students' understanding of recently discussed material.
- *Think-Pair-and-Square cooperative learning groups* go a step farther by having the first pair of students present its answer to a second pair of students.
- *A Jigsaw exercise* requires more preparation on the part of the instructor. Each group is given part of the information necessary to understand or analyze an economic issue or problem. One group may have one or two pieces of economic data. Another group has different pieces of information. The individual groups work on understanding the information that they have and then meet with another group to teach them about their information and to learn the information the second group possesses. The different pieces of the puzzle are compiled and put together until everyone has the requisite information to do the analysis.
- *Consensus building* is another cooperative learning activity. This technique is particularly good for classroom discussions of an economic issue. Students are put into groups to answer questions or to react to readings. Once a group comes to a consensus or answer, the recorder writes down the group's response and waits for the opportunity to present it to the larger class. After hearing the individual group reports, the class engages in further discussion to reach consensus. These represent rare teachable moments when an entire class of students has the background to get the most out of any insight the instructor may have to offer them.
- *Cooperative writing* takes a variety of forms from pairing up and critiquing the work of another student, to actually writing a group paper. In writing a group paper, students would meet to brainstorm and then divide up paragraphs or sections of the paper. When they meet again, drafts would be passed around to other team members of the group for comment and suggestions. All of the sections would then be compiled and re-circulated among team members for additional revisions.

Individual instructors can modify these activities depending upon the desired educational outcome, the number of students in a class, and the amount of time that can be devoted to the effort. The role of the instructor is no longer one of only covering the material but rather one of clarifying the educational task, explaining its significance to the students, deciding upon group structure, monitoring group activity, and evaluating individual and group efforts. For examples of these cooperative learning techniques, see Bartlett (1998).

III. TEAMS: THE NEXT ITERATION IN ECONOMICS

A growing number of organizations use teams to conduct business (Mohrman, Cohen, and Mohrman, 1995; Senge, Kleiner, Roberts, Ross, and Smith, 1994). Teams increase an organization's productivity through the synergy that is created by well-performing teams (Buchholz and Roth, 1987; Larson and LaFasto, 1989; Kaagan, 1999). For example, many businesses use teams of technicians, designers, and marketers to develop new products. Government legislators use teams of lawyers, experts, and writers to craft legislation. Cancer patients use a team of healthcare professionals to make important medical decisions. The world has become too complex and interconnected for individuals to possess and process all the information necessary to make good decisions or to create successful projects on their own. Consequently, to model the workings of the real world, most major business schools use teams in their courses as an integral component of the curriculum. These business schools recognize that the pedagogy used as well as the content is fundamental. Nilson (2003) observes:

> Every class conveys two lessons: one in the content and another in the teaching method. Student-active techniques send the message that with expert guidance, learners can actively discover, analyze, and use knowledge on their own. With this particular "empowerment," students come to understand that they must assume responsibility for their own learning (p. 127).

The roles that instructors have their students play, particularly with respect to teams, mimic those used in the real world. Team meetings resemble business meetings, cooperative business meetings. Students accept various leadership roles, produce agendas for their meetings, and write up the minutes of their meetings. There are three basic roles for students to play: coordinator, recorder, and facilitator. The coordinator is responsible for setting up meeting times, places, and supplying all necessary materials for the meeting. The coordinator writes up the previously agreed upon agenda and distributes it to team members along with the minutes of the last meeting before the next meeting. The recorder takes down the minutes of the meeting and supplies an edited copy to the coordinator to distribute before the next team meeting. These roles should be rotated among team members.

In the classroom, facilitators conduct the meeting and need to develop the skills necessary to efficiently conduct the meeting and to get the most from each member of the team. This means that the facilitator has to be reminded that each student has a different learning style. Some students are auditory; others are visual, tactile, or verbal learners. In team meetings, if a student does not understand a concept, rather than repeating the explanation in the same style, the facilitator may ask if someone can explain the idea in a different style.

It is critical that instructors using cooperative learning assignments and teams explain or provide written materials to the class on the potential benefits from being a member of a well-functioning team and the importance of an under-standing of different learning styles to that functioning. Team exercises are good for developing confidence and trust between team members. A short handout on learning styles and a brief test that students can complete to assess their learning styles and share with the group will help meetings run more smoothly. A sample agenda and a list of tips on how to conduct a meeting sets a tone for the meetings and keeps students on track. Finally, peer assessment and self-assessment instruments provide the instructor with the necessary information to monitor the teams. Nilson (2003) provided several examples of team assessment instruments for the classroom.[1] Teams go through stages. First, they need to bond or become familiar with each other. As they begin to work with each other there will be conflict and frustration. Early self- and peer-assessment information gives the instructor an opportunity to provide group processing information and to help teams appreciate their strengths and weaknesses and how to work with them. This is the critical step in forming a well-functioning team. Having teams write out contracts with each other, such as arriving on time and being focused, helps them set group norms. Once teams get through the norming stage, they begin to get synergistic effects.

The cooperative learning teams that I originally employed (Bartlett, 1995) were simple variations of cooperative learning groups. I took into account the fact that some students prefer to learn alone and others prefer to learn in a group. In my courses, students had a choice of working alone or working as a member of a team, so team participation was voluntary. Teams voluntarily formed at any time during the course and remained together for the duration of the term. Teams performed all of the assignments and took all of the tests as a unit. Any interaction with the instructor was also made as a team. The only safety valve, or out, for students who were unhappy with their team, was the final exam/project. Team members could take the final individually, if they so chose. Surprisingly, only one team ever split up at the final.

Students who chose to learn alone for the whole term earned a grade based upon their own performance on the various assignments. Students who chose to be on a team received a grade based upon the performance of one of their teammates on the same assignments. The teammate who performed each of the assignments was randomly selected to discourage the free-rider problem. The task could be taking a quiz, answering a problem set question, or taking an exam for the team. Although the educational tasks performed by teams were still defined by the instructor, students learned from each other and prepared for the tasks as a team. The roles that individual students played were negotiated with other team members. The team's game plan and the series of interactions among the team members were defined and negotiated by the students themselves. Normally, by the end of the semester, about 75 percent of the students chose to be on a team.

Unlike in economics, teams are a more common teaching technique in business programs at both the undergraduate and masters levels. Business programs focus on teams from the top down. Instructors team teach and students team learn, all in an effort to model the team decision-making process frequently used in the for-profit and not-for-profit worlds. There are seminars and workshops on how to become a good team leader, how to be a good team player, and how to make your team a high-performance team. Much can be learned from the business schools' use of teams.[2]

Currently, I am requiring all of my students to be on a team. The following are examples of courses recently taught that rely heavily upon structured teams.

Example One: Introductory Macroeconomics and Microeconomics

Using teams in introductory macroeconomics is cost efficient in terms of the tradeoff between the number of tests to be graded and the amount of time it takes to write up exercises and give feedback. Using teams is effective because of their synergistic effects. Although the material covered in class and by the textbook is the same as in traditional courses, the time spent in the classroom covering and working with the material is different for both the instructor and the students. For the instructor, the first day is spent going over the syllabus, explaining to students why teams are being used, and then conducting a team-building exercise. Students are randomly put into teams of four using a fishbowl filled with ping-pong balls numbered 1 through N with N being the number of students on the roster. To get the teams functioning quickly, the following exercise is conducted, illustrating that two heads are better than one, four is an improvement, and the class as a whole is even better. The example also illustrates diminishing returns to the variable input as well as the scientific method.

For this exercise the instructor should select an item that he or she and the students are very familiar with and use every day. Currency is always good for this purpose, especially in economics. Pass out a sheet of paper that has four columns on it, labeled Individual Student, Two Students, Four Students, and The Class. Ask students to take two minutes to write down in the first column every physical attribute of a penny that they can remember. After two minutes ask students to call out the number of attributes that they had written down on their sheets of paper. Write the numbers on the board. Next give the students two more minutes to work with the person next to them to come up with an expanded list in column two. After two minutes have the students call out how many attributes the two of them have identified. Write those numbers on the board. Usually, the number of identified attributes of a penny increases as students share their knowledge of a penny. Now ask students to form groups of four and expand the list even further for another two minutes. Have them call out the number of attributes of a penny that they have identified now. Write the numbers on the board. Typically, only one or two more attributes will be identified. Finally, have the class act as a whole group and call out the different attributes that they have all identified. One or two new ones may surface. Be sure that each student agrees with what has been mentioned. Now ask students to take a penny out of their pockets and look at it closely. Finally, ask them to determine how many of the attributes that they have identified are accurate.

This exercise does several things. First, students get to know the other students in their group and get to work with them. Second, the exercise demonstrates that two heads are better than one, four are better, and that if the class works as a whole a more complete picture of a penny is drawn. In addition, each student gains some confidence because each of them probably contributed some bit of knowledge about a penny. The exercise also shows how the scientific method works, as students hypothesize about the physical attributes of a penny and then empirically test their claims. Finally, observations about the knowledge of a penny that students have is equivalent to the knowledge that students bring to class each day from their own experiences and from their own studying of the material in the book. Students learn that they can contribute and make a difference in a group. They also learn that groups can take them farther than they might go alone.

The rest of the semester's classes consist of lecture for the first 20 to 30 minutes, students working through a cooperative learning exercise in their groups for the next 20 to 30 minutes, and then random selection of one group to present its answer in front of the class for questions and discussion. Few economists think they need instruction on how to lecture, but giving a mini-lecture requires instructors to get to the point quickly. Writing the cooperative learning exercises is not much different than giving students one problem from a problem set to focus on. The problem, however, should follow directly from the lecture that was just presented. The groups can congregate in different sections of the classroom and work through the exercise. The exercise would create a very teachable moment when every student had grappled with the material and could get the most out of any ensuing discussion. The answers or responses from each group are then turned in to the instructor. Once a group is selected to present its answer, one member from the group is randomly selected to come to the front of the class and demonstrate the team's answer. (The fish bowl and ping-pong balls are helpful here, too). The last 20 minutes of the class is a good opportunity to clarify any remaining questions students may have. The answers that were handed in can be graded or just glanced over to evaluate how much the class understands. Grading them is not much work because there is only one problem and one response for every four students. This teaching technique is really good for large introductory economics classes.

In this approach, the same amount of textbook material is covered as in a traditional course. However, students are expected to cover more of that material on their on or with their team outside of class, either in face-to-face meetings or in cyber meetings. Too often in traditional classrooms, instructors have a tendency to do the work for students, in effect to carry their backpacks on the journey. Instructors go over every detail in the textbook. If students understand the lecture material better by immediately working through a follow-up problem, they will be better equipped to work on the remaining problems in the book individually or as a team. It is better to cover fewer concepts in class and to make sure that students have a deep understanding of them. This combination of traditional lecture and teamwork gives students an opportunity to take more responsibility for their own learning, including being responsible for more of the material that is in the textbook and lectures.

The graded exercises from the in-class teamwork count for 40 percent of a student's grade. The combined scores on three hourly exams and a final count for the remainder of each student's grade. Dropping and adding affects team composition. A student who drops the class makes his or her team smaller. The downside for the team is that it lost a resource. The plus side is that scheduling becomes easier. Adding students gives additional resources to a team. The downside is that the team has one more person to coordinate schedules with and to assimilate into their work routines. The pluses and minuses do not always balance out. If the teams have formed and have established an identity, new students should be carefully placed.

Example Two: Teams in an Advanced Seminar

This example is from an advanced senior seminar on forensic economics, limited to 16 students, which allows for four teams of four students. Students use Martin and Vavoulis (2003) *Estimating Economic Damages* as a textbook and reference. The course is conducted as a workshop to demonstrate different aspects of estimating the economic worth of an individual. Teams agree upon a name for their group and design stationery with which to communicate with the instructor. For example, one team chose the name of "AccuFEE, Inc." for the name of its team firm.

A sample case is used throughout the semester for demonstration purposes. The students will work on their case for three-quarters of the semester. Each day I display a spreadsheet with the sample client's demographic and economic variables and all of the calculations on discounted present value to date are displayed on a screen in the front of the classroom. When new material is introduced, such as personal consumption expenditure deductions, I discuss and then demonstrate how the new information will affect the previous calculations. The data that I use for the sample case is five years older than the data required for each firm's case. As a result, each firm (team) must find its own information and make its own calculations. They are given the next 20 minutes in class to do this.

Each firm has a case, Meredith, Mark, Marianne, or Mike Davis. The Davises differ only by their race or gender. If the topic of the day is determining base earnings, students are given a sheet of paper that asks them to decide which base earnings method they will use and why. They are also asked to give the pros and cons of using each method. It is impossible for the members of the firms to do the calculations and answer the questions on the exercise in 20 minutes unless they have read all the assigned reading before class. After each firm has made its calculations and answered any questions about the appropriateness of its choices, it is given 10 minutes to demonstrate, lecture, or discuss its findings and con-clusions with the class. The instructor selects a number from one to four to randomly choose the student who will present the firm's work to the class.

Student presentations uncover interesting race and gender impacts on wrongful death calculations.

The final quarter of the course is spent estimating the economic worth of a dog and cat kennel business. Although the textbook contains no information on how to evaluate the economic worth of a business, the students use the knowledge that they have gained from working on the economic worth of individuals to think about how to go about this process. They need to determine what information they will need, plus how they will calculate the net discounted present value of the kennel. The case uses real documents of revenues and cost data from a local kennel. Teams familiarize themselves with the specifics of the case during the first week of the project and write a letter to the kennel owners for any additional information they might need.

After a week of data gathering and calculating, each firm presents a poster presentation of its findings. The 80-minute class period is divided into two sessions. During the first session, students of two of the teams evaluate the presentations of the two other teams, discussing with the presenting teams why they used certain numbers and performed certain calculations. In the last half of the session, the roles are reversed. Students who previously presented their work now will evaluate the work of the other two firms. The remaining class period of the second week is spent debating and coming to a class consensus on how best to approach the problem and then actually executing it.

The next week class teams from each section challenge each other's work by making PowerPoint presentations of their agreed-upon worth of the kennel to an unbiased, outside evaluator. Members of each team are selected to present their case: the assumptions that they made, the data that they used, and the calculations they performed. The evaluator listens to each team's case and then ranks them. Members of the team that the evaluator ranked as having the best presentation received a half grade higher on their final project grade. The last day of class was spent discussing the course, debriefing their experiences on teams, and soliciting suggestions for improving the course.

Students are graded on the case that they worked on for the three-quarters of the semester and the kennel case that they worked on for the last quarter of the semester. The continuing case counts for one-third of a student's grade and the grade is determined by the written documents that each firm turns in each class period and the final product. The kennel case counts one-third of a student's grade and is a combination of grades for the firm's write-up, poster presentation, and discussion during the final two weeks. Finally, each student's self-assessment and the team member assessment of each student's contribution to the group's learning and projects count an additional third of the student's grade. Here is where there can be considerable individual differences in grades and thus final grades. Peers reward students who contribute and make an effort in class and in their team meetings. Slackers pay the price.

The examples from these two classes can be adapted for most courses in the economics curriculum. With these approaches, fewer concepts may be covered in class, but students have the opportunity to work with an idea when it is fresh in their minds with peers who have the same goal in mind that they do – to do well in the course.

IV. DO'S AND DON'TS

The following is a composite list of do's and don'ts for cooperative learning.

Do's
- Do be sure that students know exactly what they are to do in groups and individually. The instructions for each assignment or activity should be clear, including exactly what the group is going to do, how long the group has to do the exercise, and what the group is expected to produce at the end of the time frame.
- Do make sure that students know why they are doing the task from an economic and pedagogical standpoint. Tell students why the economic principle is of interest and how this particular cooperative learning exercise will help them learn about it.
- Do decide how groups will be formed before coming to class.
- Do walk around the room and listen to student conversations during the exercises.
- Do give students enough time to reflect on the material or perform the task.
- Do give comments or suggestions when needed to facilitate the group process.
- Do make sure that the end product is meaningful and can be evaluated.
- Do use names to identify teams and build rapport.
- Do encourage students to give constructive feedback and to make helpful suggestions to other students.
- Do be encouraging and supportive.

Don'ts
- Don't use more than your allotted time in lectures, cutting group time short.
- Don't answer a question the minute you are asked. If you answer questions immediately, students will listen to the other student's question and your answer and will not reflect on the material or formulate their own questions. If you have asked the class to work on something, reserve questions until the end of the allotted time.
- Don't be too quick to bail students out yourself. If a group member gets stuck, randomly pick a member of another group and let that student give the question a try.
- Don't let students who have not done the requisite preparations free ride. Periodically have them hand in group or team assessments of their peers.
- Don't let any group have more than the allotted time to answer the question.

V. THE EVOLUTION OF TEACHING TECHNOLOGIES

The obstacles to incorporating cooperative learning exercises into economics classrooms range from "If it isn't broken …" to "The benefits do not outweigh the costs." The first obstacle is a matter of education and promotion. The second obstacle is harder to counter. Ten years ago, without the abundance of teaching technologies that are now available – from smart classrooms to instructional computer labs – the communication and management costs were very high.

Technology has made incorporating cooperative learning techniques into the economics classroom easier. The increased use of computer technology allows for more complex simulations of economic activity and access to the latest information from primary sources through the Internet, and course management software, such as WebCT and Blackboard, provides virtual meeting spaces for student teams. Email provides students with a readily accessible communication venue on most campuses for organizing meetings, exchanging contact information, and conducting virtual meetings in a timely fashion.

Instructors are able to track student use of assignments, discussions, and use of course materials more effectively and efficiently with course management software. E-classrooms are more prevalent, as are handheld personal digital assistants, creating more possibilities for simulations, experiments, and demonstrations by students. Students can show the products of their outside work by bringing them to class on a CD or access them through campus-wide shared storage space operated by the institution's computer center. More classrooms are being equipped with desks that allow students to use their personal computers either wirelessly or with jacks. Some classrooms have a desk in front of a plasma TV display with a wireless keyboard and mouse to allow students to work cooperatively as group. Bruffee (2003) and Graetz and Goliber (2002) discuss the importance of widely using cooperative learning activities and having the appropriate environment within which to conduct collaborative learning exercises on college campuses. For example, the mobility of the people, furniture and technology are important elements of the learning environment; immobility can impede learning. Group computer stations are designed specifically for this purpose. Group workstations are the standard in most business schools. Finally, most universities now have information technology and computer specialists whose sole job is to help faculty to incorporate technology into their teaching. Technology has given cooperative learning enthusiasts new ways to construct the various elements of a good cooperative learning exercise. More importantly, the cost of using cooperative learning is decreasing for the instructor, making it an attractive alternative to "chalk and talk."

NOTES

[1] Nilson's (2003) assessment instruments are more extensive than the one found in Figure

3.1. The reader, however, can easily modify Nilson's instruments for his/her own particular course.

² A simple Google web search using the keywords of teams and education will bring up Harvard University, Babson University, Rice University, and many other business schools that have team learning centers and/or recently conducted conferences on the subject.

REFERENCES

Adedayo, O. A. 1998. Differential effectiveness by gender of instructional methods on achievement in mathematics at tertiary level. *Educational Studies in Mathematics* 37 (1): 83–91.

Astin, A. W. 1993. *What Matters in College: Four Critical Years Revisited*. San Francisco: Jossey-Bass.

Bartlett, R. L. 1998. Making cooperative learning work in economics classes. In W. E. Becker, and M. Watts, eds., *Teaching Economics to Undergraduates: Alternatives to Chalk and Talk*. Cheltenham, UK: Edward Elgar: 11–34.

———. 1995. A flip of the coin -- A roll of the die: An answer to the free-rider problem in economic education. *Journal of Economic Education* 26 (2): 131–39.

Becker, W. E., and M. Watts. 2001a. Teaching economics in the 21st century: Still chalk and talk. *American Economic Review* 91 (2): 446–51.

———. 2001b. Teaching methods in U. S. undergraduate economics courses. *Journal of Economic Education* 32 (3): 269–79.

———. eds. 1998. *Teaching Economics to Undergraduates: Alternatives to Chalk and Talk*. Cheltenham, UK: Edward Elgar.

———. 1996. Chalk and talk: A national survey on teaching undergraduate economics. *American Economic Review* 86 (2): 448–53.

———. 1995. A review of teaching methods in undergraduate economics. *Economic Inquiry* 33 (4): 692–700.

Blignaut, R. J., and I. M. Venter. 1998. Teamwork: Can it equip university science students with more than rigid subject knowledge? *Computers & Education* 31: 265–79.

Brooks, T. J., and A. W. Khandker. 2002. A collaborative learning lab: Does the form matter? *Contemporary Economic Policy* 20 (3): 330–38.

Bruffee, K. A. 1993. *Collaborative Learning: Higher Education, Interdependence, and the Authority of Knowledge*. Baltimore: The Johns Hopkins University Press.

———. 2003. Cultivating the craft of interdependence: Collaborative learning and the college curriculum. *About Campus* 7 (6): 17–23.

Buchholz, S., and T. Roth. 1987. *Creating the High-Performance Team*. New York: John Wiley & Sons, Inc.

Cabrera, A. F., J. L. Crissman, E. M. Bernal, A. Nora, P. T. Terenzini, and E. T. Pascarella. 2002. Collaborative learning: Its impact on college students' development and diversity. *Journal of College Student Development* 43 (1): 20–34.

Cohn, C. L. 1999. Cooperative learning in a macroeconomics course: A team simulation. *College Teaching* 47 (2): 51–54.

Committee on Undergraduate Science Education. 1997. *Science Teaching Reconsidered: A Handbook.* National Research Council. Washington, DC: National Academies Press.

Cox, A. J., and W. F. Junkin. 2002. Enhanced student learning in the introductory physics laboratory. *Physics Education* 37 (1): 37–44.

Duncan, H., and T. Dick. 2000. Collaborative workshops and student academic performance in introductory college mathematics courses: A study of a Treisman model math Excel program. *School Science and Mathematics* 100 (7): 365–73.

Ginorio, A. B. 1995. *Warming the Climate for Women in Academic Science.* Washington, DC: Project on the Status of women, Association of American Colleges.

Giordano, P. J., and E. Y. Hammer. 1999. In-class collaborative learning: Practical suggestions from the teaching trenches. *Teaching of Psychology* 26 (1): 42–44.

Graetz, K. A., and M. J. Goliber. 2002. Designing collaborative learning places: Psychological foundations and new frontiers. *New Directions for Teaching and Learning* 92 (Winter): 13–22.

Hansen, E. J., and J. A. Stephens. 2000. The ethics of learner-centered education. *Change* 33 (5): 40–47.

Ingram, S., and A. Parker. 2002. Gender and modes of collaboration in an engineering classroom: A profile of two women on student teams. *Journal of Business and Technical Communication* 16 (1): 33–68.

Johnson, D. W., and R. T. Johnson. 1999. Making cooperative learning work. *Theory into Practice* 38 (2): 67–73.

———. 1989. *Cooperation and Competition: Theory and Research.* Edina, MN: Interaction Book Company.

Johnson, D. W., R. T. Johnson, and E. J. Holubec. 1993. *Circles of Learning: Cooperation in the Classroom.* Edina, MN: Interaction Book Company.

Johnson, D. W., R. T. Johnson, and K. A. Smith. 1991a. *Active Learning: Cooperation in the College Classroom.* Edina, MN: Interaction Book Company.

———. 1991b. Cooperative learning: Increasing college faculty instructional productivity. *ASHE-ERIC Higher Education Report* No. 4. Washington, DC: The George Washington University, School of Education and Human Development.

Johnston, C. G., R. H. James, J. N. Lye, and I. M. McDonald. 2000. An evaluation of collaborative problem solving for learning economics. *Journal of Economic Education* 31 (1): 13–29.

Kaagan, S. S. 1999. *Leadership Games: Experiential Learning for Organizational Development.* Thousand Oaks, CA: SAGE Publications, Inc.

Kagan, S. 1994. *Cooperative Learning.* San Juan Capistrano, CA: Kagan Cooperative Learning.

Keenan, D., and M. H. Maier. 1994. *Economics Live!: Learning Economics the Collaborative Way.* New York: McGraw-Hill.

Khandker, A. W., and A. Elfessi. 2000.Teaching introductory microeconomics with an in-class collaborative learning lab. *Journal of Economics* 26 (2): 59–71.

Larson, C. E., and F. M. J. LaFasto. 1989. *TeamWork: What Must Go Right, What Can Go Wrong.* Newbury Park, CA: SAGE Publications, Inc.

Maier, M. H. 2001. Reporting out: Closure without the tedium. *Journal of Cooperation & Collaboration in College Teaching* 10 (3): 117–21.

Maier, M. H., and D. Keenan. 1994. Cooperative learning in economics. *Economic Inquiry* 32 (April): 358–61.

Manzer, J. P., and D. M. Bialik. 1997. Team and group learning strategies for business and economics classes. *Business Education Forum* 51 (4): 32–35.

Martin, G. D., and T. Vavoulis. 2003. *Determining Economic Damages*. Costa Mesa, California: James.

McCarthy, J. P., and L. Anderson. 2000. Active learning techniques versus traditional teaching styles: Two experiments from history and political science. *Innovative Higher Education* 24 (4): 279–94.

Meyers, C., and T. B. Jones. 1993. *Promoting Active Learning: Strategies for the Classroom*. San Francisco: Jossey-Bass.

Miglietti, C. 2002. Using cooperative small groups in introductory accounting classes: A practical approach. *Journal of Education for Business* 78 (2): 111–15.

Miller, N., and H. J. Harrington. 1990. A situational identity perspective on cultural diversity and teamwork in the classroom. In S. Sharan, ed., *Cooperative Learning: Theory and Research*. New York: Praeger: 39–75.

Mohrman, S. A., S. G. Cohen, and A. M. Mohrman, Jr. 1995. *Designing Team-Based Organizations: New Forms for Knowledge Work*. San Francisco: Jossey-Bass.

Moore, R. L. 1998. Teaching introductory economics with a collaborative learning lab component. *Journal of Economic Education* 29 (4): 321–29.

Nilson, L. B. 2003. Learning in groups. *Teaching at Its Best: A Research-Based Resource for College Instructors*. Bolton, MA: Anker: 125–36.

Nordstrom, K. F. 1996. Assessment of collaborative approaches to teaching an undergraduate environmental management course. *Journal of Geography* 95 (5): 213–21.

Potthast, M. J. 1999. Outcomes of using small-group cooperative learning experiences in introductory statistics courses. *College Student Journal* 33 (1): 34–42.

Qin, Z., D. Johnson, and R. T. Johnson. 1995. Cooperative versus competitive efforts and problem solving. *Review of Educational Research* 65 (2): 129–43.

Scearce, C. 1992. *100 Ways to Build Teams*. Palatine, IL: IRI/Skylight Training and Publishing.

Schmidt, S. J. 2003. Active and cooperative learning using web-based simulations. *Journal of Economic Education* 34 (2): 151–67.

Senge, P. M., A. Kleiner, C. Roberts, R. B. Ross, and B. J. Smith. 1994. *The Fifth Discipline Fieldbook: Strategies and Tools for Building a Learning Organization*. New York: Doubleday.

Sharan, S. 1990. *Cooperative Learning: Theory and Research*. New York: Praeger.

Slavin, R. E. 1999. Comprehensive approaches to cooperative learning. *Theory into Practice* 38 (2): 74–9.

————. 1990. *Cooperative Learning: Theory, Research, and Practice*. Needham Heights, MA: Allyn and Bacon.

Stein, R. F., and S. Hurd. 2000. *Using Student Teams in the Classroom: A Faculty Guide*. Bolton, MA: Anker.

Treisman, U. 1992. Studying students studying calculus: A look at the lives of minority mathematics students in college. *The College Mathematics Journal* 23 (5): 362–72.

Vaughan, W. 2002. Effects of cooperative learning on achievement and attitude among students of color. *The Journal of Educational Research* 95 (6): 359–64.

Vik, G. N. 2001. Doing more to teach teamwork than telling students to sink or swim. *Business Communication Quarterly* 64 (4): 112–19.

White, F. C. 1997. An interactive learning system for the economic analysis of public policies. *Journal of Economic Education* 28 (3): 222–29.

Williams, R. B. 1993. *More than 50 Ways to Build Team Consensus*. Palatine, IL: IRI/Skylight Training and Publishing.

Yuan, R., and S. Benson. 2000. Teamwork and research at the frontiers of learning. *New Directions for Higher Education* 109 (Spring): 51–57.

Zimbardo, P. G., L. D. Butler, and V. A. Wolfe. 2003. Cooperative college examinations: More gain, less pain when students share information and grades. *Journal of Experimental Education* 71 (2): 101–25.

CHAPTER 4

USING THE CASE METHOD IN THE ECONOMICS CLASSROOM

John A. Carlson

Ann Velenchik

Imagine an economics class in which students do most of the talking. Is that a waste of class time? Are they likely to learn much economics in the process? Many economists may be surprised with our assertion that such classes can be structured so that students do in fact learn a lot of economics. The structure we have in mind is known as the case method.

When we talk about the case method, we are referring to an active learning technique that uses classroom discussion of a written narrative, or case, as a strategy for developing students' analytical tools and skills. The cases used for teaching are not "case studies" of the sort used in academic research; that is, they do not explicitly apply analytical methods or techniques, they do not generally reach conclusions, and they do not evaluate the quality of the policies or decisions they describe. The goal is to use a case to help students learn economics rather than to teach about a particular example or event. To keep this distinction clear, we refer to the "case method" rather than the "case study method" throughout this chapter.

In previous work (Carlson and Schodt, 1995; Velenchik, 1995) we have written at some length about the advantages and costs of the case method. (See also Boehrer, 1991; Christensen and Hansen, 1987; Buckles, 1999, and references cited by those authors.) The advantages of the case method come in the degree of engagement of students with the cases and thus with the economic ideas in them, in the new energy that pedagogical variety brings to the classroom, and in what we see of our students' ability to apply the economics they are learning and to work with data. The costs occur in the faculty time it takes to identify good cases, integrate them in the syllabus and prepare and teach them, and in the material that must be sacrificed in order to incorporate them into a course. After a dozen years of experience, we both believe the benefits far outweigh the costs and continue to use cases in our teaching.

Our own forays into the use of the case method began when we both participated in the Pew Faculty Fellowship in International Affairs. The Pew Fellowship was a two-week residential training program at Harvard University intended to expand the use of the case method in college-level instruction in international affairs. The program was offered for five years, and brought together faculty members from several disciplines and a wide range of colleges and universities. There were five economists in our group, and about 20 economists over the Pew Fellowship's history.

We begin with a guide to using the case method, focusing on three basic steps: first, selecting cases and integrating them into the syllabus; second, preparing students for their roles with the case method; and third, conducting the classroom discussion. We then provide and discuss three examples of cases, drawn from our own experiences, and conclude with a list of do's and don'ts. We consulted with eight other economist alumni of the Pew program as we prepared this chapter and its concluding list, so the advice is drawn from their experiences as well as ours.

I. INTRODUCING THE CASE METHOD: A PRIMER

Step One: Integrating Cases into the Syllabus

We, and the colleagues we surveyed, have had experience using cases across the economics curriculum, in principles, intermediate theory, econometrics, and electives at all levels, in both undergraduate and graduate courses. Based on that experience, we believe that the method can be incorporated in virtually any college-level economics course. Although it is difficult to use the method in extremely large classes, we know instructors who have used it in a class of more than 100 students, and we have found it manageable, if not ideal, in classes with 35 to 45 students. The first tasks in using the case method are deciding where, why, and how frequently to use cases, and then choosing which cases to use. There is a certain degree of simultaneity in these choices, because the availability of good cases on particular subjects may drive the selection of what issues to teach using cases and the number of cases to include in the course.

Although it is possible to teach a course using the case method exclusively, as is done at some business schools, we find that most economists who use cases employ them as one of a number of pedagogical techniques and continue to lecture as an important way of delivering new material. When we asked our Pew economist colleagues about their case use, they reported using cases in a range from 10 to 50 percent of class meetings, with a clear mode at about 25 percent. Most instructors devote the entire class meeting to a case, but three reported that they also do mini-cases that can take as little as 10 or 15 minutes. Because effective use of cases requires learning about the method on the part of both teachers and students, we suggest that instructors using the case method for the first time plan on incorporating at least two or three cases in a course in order to allow participants to become comfortable with the method.

The process of introducing cases in a course begins with a review of the syllabus to identify material that can be taught effectively with cases. Cases can be used for several purposes. They can motivate new material, introduce theoretical concepts or empirical methods, or be used as empirical examples or applications to reinforce the learning of theory. Cases work best when there is a specific well-defined pedagogical goal, so part of the work that goes into selecting and incorporating cases is the careful definition of what one is trying to teach and how the case is going to enhance that learning.

How the case is to be used will determine its placement in the syllabus and the kinds of cases that are appropriate. For example, cases used to motivate instruction on an issue are best when they help students appreciate the need for a theoretical framework or empirical tools to develop good answers to the questions posed by the case. Cases that are designed to teach theory, which is the most challenging application of the method, should be focused on solving a well-defined problem, giving students the chance to arrive at a solution technique during the classroom discussion.[1] Cases used as applications work best when they require students to choose which theoretical concepts or empirical tools are most appropriate, forcing students to think deeply about the analytical tools they have learned and the types of questions they can address. These cases can be introduced after the theoretical framework has been presented to the class. We recommend employing a mix of these different uses for cases to avoid predictable and potentially boring patterns of instruction.

One method of incorporating cases in the syllabus is to choose which subjects to cover with cases, and then find appropriate cases on those topics. Two good sources for published cases are the Harvard Business School <http://harvardbusinessonline.hbsp.harvard.edu/> and the Kennedy School of Government <http://ksgcase.harvard.edu/>. Both web sites allow searches by subject matter and provide good descriptions of cases. Instructors should read the entire case to evaluate what it will add to a course before selecting it for classroom use.

A second strategy is to locate cases that are relevant for the course you are teaching, and then build them into the syllabus. Many published cases can be used for more than one purpose. For example, after seeing Debora Spar of the Harvard Business School teach her case entitled "Hitting the Wall: Nike and International Labor Practices," (Spar and Burns, 2000) to a group of Wellesley social science faculty, the second author added it to the syllabus of her seminar in economic development, using it as a way to talk about the issue of fair wages. Other faculty members who attended Spar's presentation have incorporated the case in courses in ethics and on the role of non-governmental organizations in influencing policy. The teaching of the case varies across courses, as each instructor designs questions and leads discussions to emphasize particular ideas. The key thing is that the instructor gives serious thought to what he or she is trying to teach and how this case helps to do it, keeping that purpose in mind when the case is selected and when it is taught.

There are some general characteristics of effective cases, regardless of the topic or the use (introduction, motivation, application). Cases vary in style, length and complexity, but it is best to choose those that are not especially long. Students must work closely with the material in order to prepare for the class. Excessive length can be quite daunting to them and interfere with their gaining detailed knowledge of the facts of the case that makes for good discussion. Fifteen pages of text seems to us to be the maximum effective length. Ideally, the case allows students to hone their ability to use data by including quantitative information of varying degrees of relevance (including potentially irrelevant data) presented in a range of forms (tables, charts, graphs). The data should require some interpretation in order to be useful. Decision-forcing cases, in which the protagonist is an economic actor who must make a choice and act, tend to engage students most easily. These cases have the additional advantage of being set in rich political and social contexts, helping students understand the complexity of policymaking.

All of the economists we contacted use published cases from some established sources but most of them also rely on cases they have researched and written themselves. Articles from the media – including newspapers, magazines, and the transcripts of radio and television stories – can be used individually as sources or combined into longer cases. Although cases are usually drawn from actual events, it is not especially important that they be extremely current. Indeed, four of our colleagues report that they still frequently use a case about the Harley Davidson Motorcycle Company that was published in 1986 and recounts events that took place in the 1970s and early 1980s. (Robyn, 1986). A good case for understanding the gold standard involves a decision facing Britain in 1925 (Rukstad, 1992).

What is important is that the case be engaging and information rich; it should not contain analysis of the problems or issues presented, but leave that for students to do. On occasion, materials for cases appear serendipitously. The first example of a case in this chapter was inspired when a coupon was handed through a car window when the author was on her way to a vacation in Maine.

Step Two: Preparing Students
The success of the case method depends critically on student participation, and thus on student preparation. Most economics courses include relatively little of any sort of active learning technique, let alone one that is as reliant on student involvement as the case method, so it is essential to provide students with instruction in the use of the method and guidelines for preparing for each discussion. Appendix 4.1 contains the text of a handout that has been used

successfully in a number of courses. Note the emphasis placed on students reading the case several times, making notes, and organizing their thoughts around questions and themes. Effective preparation is time consuming for students, and it is helpful to convince them of the close relationship between the quality of their preparation and the quality of the discussion.

Standard practice is to give students questions to guide their preparation and encourage them to write out answers. In general, these should not be exactly the same questions used to guide the classroom discussion, because duplication can degenerate into students reading prepared answers, which is not engaging and does not lead to student interaction. The questions should be designed to focus students' reading, helping them to identify important questions and information and begin the process of analysis. Ideally, the bulk of the thinking should take place during class discussion, generated by ideas from other students. Some questions should focus students on facts whereas others ask them to do some preliminary analysis. Published cases generally include some study questions, although we have found it useful to add questions tailored to the particular course or group of students. The examples we provide later in this chapter include sample preparation questions.

We recommend that the instructor talks with students about his or her expectations for using the case method. Explaining the purpose can encourage students to buy into the method. It is essential to discuss how (if at all) student performance will be evaluated, what the ground rules for participation are (e.g., whether the instructor will call on students who do not volunteer, how to handle follow-up questions or debates) and how the instructor will use the blackboard or other means of tracking the discussion. The more students know about the procedures and expectations, the more effectively they can participate.

Students should know what constitutes good participation and valuable contributions. A handout that presents one set of such criteria, and outlines a method for evaluating participation, is presented in Appendix 4.2.

Step Three: Leading the Discussion
One of the myths about the case method is that, because students do most of the talking, case teaching requires less faculty preparation than do lectures. Sadly, this is not true. Effective case teaching requires a great deal of preparation, beginning with mastery of all of the details of the case, both factual and analytical, including knowing where to find what information. Reading the case using the student guidelines in the handout presented in Appendix 4.1 is a good place to start.

The next step is to plan the discussion. Leading a case discussion consists of two primary activities: questioning and listening. Although every discussion is different and the instructor cannot control every aspect, it is important to have an overarching plan, particularly in terms of where he or she wants the discussion to end and what lessons students should draw from it. The instructor should be flexible enough, however, to pursue unexpected, interesting ideas that emerge from a discussion. The instructor should develop a series of questions to ask the students, and write out a list of the anticipated answers. Good discussion questions are open-ended without being vague, and specific without fishing for one particular answer. Some questions seek facts; others move students into analysis. Some questions generate lists of answers and others focus on identifying analytical steps. Some will be directed at the whole class, but others target specific students or groups of students. In the best case method classes, the second question is a natural follow-up to answers to the first question, and so on, so it can be quite useful to map out in advance a number of alternative routes through the material.

The instructor should think about whether to make use of some small group discussions or role-playing in class, and where to use it. Both can be effective tools for allowing more students to talk, generating discussion between students and helping students see alternative points of view, which is one of the most valuable attributes of using cases.

With pre-planning, the instructor controls use of the blackboard or overhead, both in terms of which questions and answers to record and how much to record. Students notice whether the instructor records what they say, and take that as an indication of the quality of their contributions, so bear that in mind. Keeping a written record helps focus the discussion, but writing too much can be distracting and time consuming for everyone. Determining the proper balance for each case takes experience.

The first step in discussing the case in class is organizing student seating in the classroom. Few instructors have the good fortune to teach in classrooms designed for case teaching, where seats are arranged in a U-shaped amphitheatre, but it helps to rearrange the student desks or chairs into a circle or semi-circle so that the students can see one another and the board or overhead and the instructor can see everyone and access the board. One of the goals of case teaching is to get students engaged in discussion with one another, as well as with the instructor. To facilitate this, provide students with cards printed with their first names that they can place upon their desks – it is surprising to note how many students don't know their classmates' names, even at small colleges.

During the discussion, the instructor acts as a guide, or a conductor, steering student responses to meet pedagogical goals and keeping the discussion moving forward by not getting bogged down in irrelevant or unnecessary details. This may involve asking the same question a number of ways, or following up with particular students to get more detail in their responses. Listening to student responses tells the instructor where to go with the next question and how to lead students to express their thoughts more clearly.

Ask students *how* they know what they know, forcing them to root their answers in the case and point out to their classmates where they found their information. Students will sometimes bring in information from outside the case, including knowledge drawn from personal experience and from outside research. This information can provide richness to the discussion, but we encourage our classes to draw their analytical conclusions based on the information available in the case itself. To get students talking with *each other*, the instructor should avoid the urge to respond to each student intervention, because that reinforces students' inclination to engage in one-on-one conversations with the teacher instead of with their classmates. Remember to pause after asking a question, giving students time to formulate answers – the silence is not nearly as dangerous to the discussion as are instructors who constantly rush to answer their own questions. Role-playing exercises, in which students are assigned to act as characters in the case, can be particularly useful for discussing cases in which there are competing interests or points of view. Making those assignments in advance is not necessary – it can be useful to divide students into groups "on the fly," based only on where they are sitting or by counting off.

During the course of the discussion, the instructor should draw in as many students as possible, including those who seem reluctant to speak, and prevent any individual student from dominating the discussion. Techniques for doing this vary a great deal among case teachers. Some instructors call on students who have not volunteered, but if they do this they must reassure students that their intent is not to embarrass them, assuming the students have read the case and prepared for class. Some instructors give extremely reluctant students an opportunity for additional preparation by telling them specific questions in advance.

We recommend assigning a brief written follow-up evaluation of each case. We often do this by allowing about five minutes for students to answer the following questions:

1. What did you learn?
2. How do you feel you performed?
3. What did you like or dislike about the case discussion?

This provides the instructor with feedback on what may or may not have resonated with the students and a sense of how involved any students felt who did not speak during a case discussion. These self-evaluations may also be used by the instructor in evaluating student performance.

II. EXAMPLE ONE: TOLL DISCOUNTS ON THE MAINE TURNPIKE

The second author (Ann Velenchik) has frequently used the following case on the first day of her microeconomics principles course at Wellesley, after the usual attendance taking and syllabus distribution. It concerns a policy experiment in Maine in which the Turnpike Authority offered discounts on tolls to motorists using the highway during off-peak hours. The case is used to motivate learning many topics in the principles course, including opportunity cost, downward sloping demand, demand elasticity, congestion externalities, and the use of data to guide policy decisions. Class discussions return to this example many times over the semester, so in addition to providing real-world relevance and motivation for the course, it becomes a nice organizing framework. Students are given a page containing photocopies of a coupon and survey that was distributed to drivers entering the Maine turnpike in the summer of 1995. (The reading and discussion generally take about half an hour.)

The coupon offered a discount of up to $1.60 off tolls for drivers who used the Turnpike Friday mornings and evenings and Sunday mornings and evenings during the period between the first of August and Labor Day.[2] Attached to the coupon was a single page survey that drivers were asked to complete and mail to the Turnpike Authority. The survey provided some explanation for the coupons and asked motorists to answer questions about the type of vehicle they were driving, the frequency of their Turnpike use, the purpose of their trips and the number of people in the vehicle. They were also asked to indicate whether they had used a coupon and whether and how they had changed their travel plans in order to do so. The final question asked them to consider the possibility that the Turnpike Authority might *raise* tolls during peak hours instead of offering the discount during off-peak hours. The question presented a variety of different-sized toll hikes and respondents were asked to indicate whether a hike of that size would cause them to alter their travel plans.

Students are asked to read the materials in class and jot down brief answers to the following questions, which are intended to focus their attention, and do not require any serious preparation:

1. Why did the Turnpike Authority offer this coupon?
2. Why does the survey ask about the purpose and frequency of the trip?
3. Is there any other piece of information you would like to have?

The discussion begins by asking why the Turnpike is issuing the coupon. Students are easily able to see that the idea is to give people an incentive to drive at off-peak times, and quickly get to the underlying problem of congestion at peak times. Follow-up questions focus on the issue of opportunity cost – by making it cheaper to drive at off-peak times, is the Turnpike Authority making it more expensive to drive during peak hours? Is the failure to save $1.60 the same as spending an extra $1.60? This discussion requires focused questioning and it sometimes takes some time to get students to begin to understand opportunity cost.

A second line of questioning asks students to think about the Turnpike Authority's underlying behavioral assumption about the relationship between the level of the toll and Turnpike use. Persistent questioning usually gets students to the realization that the Turnpike Authority is assuming a downward sloping demand curve.

The next question returns to the idea of opportunity cost, asking students whether they think that raising tolls in peak travel times, as suggested in the last part of the survey, would have the same effect on people's behavior, in terms of their choices about whether and when to drive the Turnpike, as would lowering tolls in off-peak times.

The fourth line of questioning concerns the survey, and asks students to think about the usefulness of the information gathered there. Getting students to focus on the purpose and frequency of travel raises the idea of the variation across individuals in the degree of their responsiveness to price incentives, and how that variation is correlated with some observable characteristics. This part of discussion ends with the idea of elasticity, but also provides an opportunity to talk about the use of data, which isn't part of many principles courses, but should be.

Finally, students are asked whether this was the kind of thing they expected to study in microeconomics. Their answers provide a nice way to establish what will be taught in the rest of the course. This short case is an effective way to begin the principles class. By focusing on traffic congestion, a real-world problem familiar to all students, and their thinking about how prices influence behavior, students begin the process of learning how economists think.

III. EXAMPLE TWO: BRAZIL 1998

In the course International Monetary Problems, offered to advanced under-graduates and masters-level students at Purdue University, the first author (John Carlson) uses cases in a historical sequence on transitions from the gold standard, to the Bretton Woods system, to general floating among major currencies. More recent cases deal with problems in Europe in 1992 leading up to the formation of the European Monetary Union and with whatever may be a hot topic in the news (such as, in different years, issues in Indonesia, Brazil, Argentina, China, and countries adopting currency boards or dollarization). Several of these cases are described by Rukstad (1992), and his instructor's manual provides detailed and useful guidelines on how he conducts each case.

One particularly effective case is based on an article that appeared in the *Wall Street Journal*, October 16, 1998, concerning what Brazil should do in light of its financial problems at the time and drawing on a number of concepts developed in the course. The protagonist in the case is Brazilian President Fernando Cardoso.

The article explains the views of Milton Friedman and other economists who argued that Brazil should let the market determine the value of the Real (the Brazilian currency). For a contrary position, the article points out the serious economic problems encountered by several countries in Southeast Asia in 1997 following major devaluations there, and quotes Robert Mundell's statement to the effect that "an exchange rate is a promise; to change it is to default on a commitment." (Wessel and Torres, 1998, p. A1)

This case comes late in the semester, after seven prior cases and considerable analysis of international financial linkages, so the discussion questions can be fairly open-ended. Students hand in answers to the following questions when they come to class:

1. Your opinion: Do you think Brazil should, at that time, have substantially devalued the Real? Yes or no? Indicate briefly the reason for your answer.
2. Write a question or comment you have about the article that you think we should talk about more fully in class.

Typically opinions are divided fairly evenly. The discussion of the case begins with students presenting facts about the Brazilian economy at the time the article was written that they can glean from the article. These include the nature of the crawling peg of 7 percent per year,[3] estimates that the Real is overvalued by 25 percent, high trade and government budget deficits, very high interest rates, international reserves down to $40 billion and falling by $10 billion a month, and high and rising unemployment. These facts, showing an economy in serious trouble, are recorded on the board.

The discussion then moves to the pros and cons of various options that Cardoso might choose. The students are discouraged from blurting out reactions and are expected to respond to each other when recognized by the instructor. In addition to points mentioned in the article, students often come up with additional ideas, particularly if they oppose a major devaluation. They might suggest increasing the rate of crawl or resorting to capital controls.

Toward the end of the class period, students are told what actually happened. Brazil held the line for almost three months until January 13, 1999, when it lowered the dollar value of the Real by 8.3 percent. Two days later, Cardoso gave up a peg completely and the market forced a 37 percent depreciation of the Real. If there is time, the class can discuss further why these changes occurred and the performance of the Brazilian economy after the changes were made. This sort of follow-up often occurs at the beginning of the next class meeting after a case discussion.

IV. EXAMPLE THREE: PEANUT POLICY

The previous two examples came from near the beginning and near the end of their respective courses. This example can be effectively taught midway through either principles or intermediate microeconomics courses. It concerns U.S. policy in the peanut market and is based on the transcript of an NPR story broadcast in January 1996. The story concerns Congressional budget debates that could potentially affect the peanut price support program. Key figures in the story include representatives of peanut growers' associations, representatives of peanut-product manufacturers' groups and a member of Congress whose New York constituents represent peanut and peanut-product consumers. The case is short (two-and-a-half typed single-space pages), but provides detail about the policy and a number of divergent points of view.

Students receive the following four questions to guide their preparation:

1. What is (was) the goal of the government's peanut program?
2. What are the elements of the government policy? That is, of what does the peanut program consist?
3. The reporter interviewed members of three groups concerned with the peanut program. Briefly summarize each group's point of view, and explain why they feel the way they do.
4. How do you think the people of Senegal, a peanut-growing country, view the U.S. peanut program?

The discussion begins with the first of the preparation questions. Although we generally do not advise using the same set of questions for preparation and discussion, teaching students to begin policy analysis with a clear statement of the policy goals makes that repetition desirable in this instance. It usually takes some time to get students to make the leap from the obvious (the goal is to maintain high peanut prices) to the idea that the goal is to maintain peanut farmers' incomes. This is an essential point to which we return later, when we discuss policy alternatives.

After the goal of the program is established, the second author (Velenchik) focuses the conversation on the details of the program. In their preparation, students have identified the three major elements of peanut policy (import restrictions, production quotas or licenses, and price supports) set out in the case. The primary analytical task during the class meeting is generating a diagrammatic representation of these three components. She frequently divides the class into three smaller groups, and assigns each one to draw a diagram showing the effect of one of the three components on the U.S. domestic price and quantity of peanuts. Representatives from each group are then called to the board to draw their diagrams. Lively discussion usually ensues and, no matter how many errors are in the original diagrams, the other students in the class have always been able to arrive ultimately at correct diagrams. We then combine all three into a single diagram that allows us to see the relative importance of each component of the peanut program and discuss the relationships among them. The diagram is used to show the effects of changes in the program elements.

This analytical framework helps guide the rest of the discussion, which focuses on assessing the effects of the policy on interested parties. A brief role play exercise serves to clarify each position, and then we discuss how one might quantify the gains and losses accruing to each party, although the case does not provide enough information to make actual welfare calculations. The final substantive point is an attempt to define alternative policies that would achieve the goal we defined at the beginning with fewer costs to other parties.

The class usually concludes with some discussion of the rhetorical devices used by speakers in the story. Part of the goal, especially in principles classes, is to help students evaluate what they hear about economic policy. The case contains quite a bit of flag-waving, appeals to jingoistic and xenophobic sentiments, and fast and loose use of economic jargon. It is interesting and helpful for students to identify these rhetorical devices and analyze the effects they have on their own reaction to the case.

V. DO'S AND DON'TS

As a summary of points developed in this chapter, we conclude with a number of do's and don'ts:

- Do encourage students to do pre-case work in groups, perhaps with a written product that they turn in for formal or informal evaluation.
- Do prepare students for cases in advance, especially with questions.
- Do walk into the classroom with a good blackboard or overhead design for leading and recording the discussion.
- Do recognize that what you choose to write on the board has meaning for students in terms of the case and their participation.
- Do allow for silence as students think about their answers.
- Do get everyone involved if at all possible.
- Do encourage students to respond directly to each other.
- Do listen carefully. It is hard to focus on listening when you are thinking about the next question, but you must hear what the student is saying, or trying to say.
- Do try to be relaxed – it helps the students relax and encourages participation.
- Do use role play and small groups to allow more students to speak and help them take strong positions.
- Do recognize that case teaching and case learning are skills that need to be honed and developed – give yourself and your students a chance to improve before deciding if the method works for you.
- Don't embarrass or shut students down. They may never volunteer again.
- Don't have an extended one-on-one conversation with a student; make the students to talk to each other.
- Don't deliberately leave anyone out of the conversation.
- Don't respond to each and every comment, and resist the urge to rephrase students' interventions.
- Don't sit or stand where you cannot see one or more of your students. If you can't see someone you aren't likely to bring them into the discussion.
- Don't think you can insert a case into an existing course without giving serious thought to what you are trying to teach and how the case will help you do that.

APPENDIX 4.1: Case Preparation Guidelines for Students

General Approach

Learning means creating your own ideas, not just accepting new information. To prepare a case effectively, you need to take an active approach, and aim for some goal beyond just knowing the case. Study it as if you needed to understand it in order to solve some problem or accomplish some objective. Ask yourself such questions as: What experience can this case help me understand? What present or future problem can it help me solve? Use the study questions to help you use the information in the case actively. Don't just read the case. Put it to work!!

Specific Steps

1. Get a sense of the whole case

Look at the case before you read it. What do the title and the heading tell you? What information do the tables, graphs and appendices present? Who are the central characters? What is the story about?

Look at the study questions. What do you want to know?

Read the case quickly, looking for the broad outlines. Identify and locate the information it presents.

2. State the issues

Ask yourself what the case is really about. What problems are the people in it dealing with? Where do you see conflict between ideas, goals, perspectives and values?

3. Organize the details

Read the case more carefully. Ask yourself which details will help you answer the study questions and your own questions.

Mark the case so you can find details later. Take notes to help you see relationships.

Ask yourself what additional information you need to complete the analysis. Although it is not necessary to go find this information, awareness of what is missing can be quite useful.

4. Determine the analysis required

Return to the study questions: What do they ask you to figure out?

Identify the analytic steps suggested by the tables, graphs and appendices.

Find an approach to take to get more meaning out of this information.

5. Do the analysis you think is worthwhile

Prepare to present, explain and justify your analysis.

6. Make something of your work

Ask yourself what you have learned from the case. Articulate answers to the questions you began with. Prepare to present and defend your conclusions.

Some questions to ask in preparing a case

What is the situation? What problem(s) need to be solved?

What else do you need to know in order to:
      identify your options?
      select an option?
      implement a particular option?

What are all the possible options? (Think creatively)

What are the costs/benefits and pros/cons of each option? (Think critically)

Who (individuals and groups) will benefit or lose from each option?

What kinds of qualitative or quantitative analysis can you apply to the situation?

What would you do? Which option would you choose?

How adequate/appropriate is your chosen option?

What criteria do you use in making this assessment?

Do you see any difference between short- and long-term effects of the option you have chosen?

What is the best outcome you can foresee from the option you propose?

What is the worst? Is there any possibility that the option you propose might make the problem worse?

What lessons can you learn from the outcomes presented in the case?

Why did the teacher assign the case? What are students supposed to learn or notice?

APPENDIX 4.2: Handout on Evaluating Participation

Although it would be impossible for me to remember all contributions, I will try to evaluate each person's participation in a case discussion on a scale from 0 to 5:

0   unexcused absence
3   less than adequate participation
4   acceptable participation
5   excellent contribution(s)

Some of what I am looking for includes:

a. Content mastery. There is an indication of careful reading of the case and an understanding of the situation. The student contributes relevant information from the case. This would be a minimum expectation for acceptable participation.

b. Contribution to process. The student's contribution demonstrates listening to others, building upon the ideas of others, responding to or providing constructive criticism of others, asking relevant questions. This would solidify an acceptable rating and in many instances will be rated excellent.

c. Quality of argument. The student's contribution demonstrates use of evidence, logical consistency, aptness to issues under discussion, originality and creativity, makes useful connections to other course materials or to prior cases. If well done, this would rate an excellent contribution.

Less than adequate participation includes being present but not speaking at all, giving only one or two word answers to questions without at least a little elaboration, making remarks that are totally irrelevant, showing insensitivity to others, or rambling incoherently.

You should try to participate even if you do not feel what you have to say meets the criteria of an acceptable contribution. You may surprise yourself. Furthermore, your question or answer may advance the discussion and clarify things in other people's minds far more than someone else's brilliant discourse. Do not hesitate to admit confusion, ask for clarification, or simply be wrong. In general, be alert to ways to keep the class discussion moving toward a solution to the case.

After the midterm, I will try to give you feedback on how I have evaluated your participation during the first few case discussions.

NOTES

[1] Schodt (2000) provides examples of cases that he has found useful for teaching economic theory.

[2] The authors will provide copies of this and the other unpublished case material mentioned in this chapter to interested readers upon request.

[3] A country with a crawling peg manages its exchange rate so that its currency depreciates steadily at a preannounced rate against another currency. In the case of the Brazilian Real, the other currency was the U.S. dollar.

REFERENCES

Boehrer, J. 1991. Spectators and gladiators: Reconnecting the students with the problem. *Teaching Excellence* 2 (7): 1–2.

Buckles, S. 1999. Using cases as an effective active learning technique. In W. E. Becker and M. Watts, eds., *Teaching Economics to Undergraduates: Alternatives to Chalk and Talk*. Cheltenham, UK: Edward Elgar, 225–40.

Carlson, J. A., and D. W. Schodt. 1995. Beyond the lecture: Case teaching and the learning of economic theory. *Journal of Economic Education* 26 (Winter):17–28.

Christensen, C. R., with A. J. Hansen. 1987. *Teaching and the Case Method*. Cambridge: Harvard Business School.

Robyn, D. 1986. *Revving Up for Relief: Harley-Davidson at the ITC*. Kennedy School of Government Case Program, Case Number C16-86-779.0. Cambridge: The President and Fellows of Harvard College.

Rukstad, M. B. 1992. *Macroeconomic Decision Making in the World Economy*. 3rd ed., Fort Worth, TX: Dryden Press.

Spar, D. and J. Burns. 2000. *Hitting the Wall: Nike and International Labor Practices*. Harvard Business School Publications Product Number 9-700-074. Cambridge: The President and Fellows of Harvard College.

Schodt, D. W. 2000. Using cases to teach analytical skills. In J. S. Lantis, L. M. Kuzma and J. Boehrer, eds. *The New International Studies Classroom: Active Teaching, Active Learning*. Boulder: Lynn Rienner, 65–76.

Velenchik, A. 1995. The case method as a strategy for teaching policy analysis to undergraduates. *Journal of Economic Education* 26 (Winter): 29–38.

Wessel, D. and C. Torres. 1998. Hard calls: Devalue? Cut Rates? Cardoso must decide between dueling experts. *Wall Street Journal*, October 16: A1.

CHAPTER **5**

USING ACTIVE LEARNING TECHNIQUES IN LARGE LECTURE CLASSES

Stephen Buckles

Gail Mitchell Hoyt

Many students take principles of economics courses in classes with more than 100 students. Some instructors who teach these classes are such dynamic and engaging speakers that they can keep their students attentive and involved in learning for an entire class period using lecture alone. Unfortunately, many instructors do not fall into that category. Learning to use a wide variety of good lecturing techniques such as providing outlines or lists of key points for class, breaking hour-long lectures into a series of mini-lectures, relating material to previous lectures and students' prior knowledge, and using current events can all help large lecture instructors be more effective. In this chapter we provide strategies that go one step beyond traditional lecturing techniques for those who want to find more ways for students to participate in learning. Although these approaches can be effective in a class of any size, there are special challenges in the large lecture class that may lead instructors to avoid learning to use them. So as we present these active learning methods we also address the challenges unique to the large lecture class.

Active learning is different from traditional lecturing styles and particularly lectures in large classrooms and in economics classes. Traditionally, faculty members do most of the work and students appear to play passive roles. Active learning requires students to do things such as read, write, talk, listen to others and respond, and apply and use content and concepts. Active learning can involve small group interaction and discussion, simulations, games, case studies, and problem solving activities. Engaging students in active learning does mean that less time remains for lecturing and a reduction in content coverage becomes one of the potential costs of the pedagogical techniques we propose. That breadth of coverage by faculty can be regained in alternative fashions. The benefit of active learning techniques is a gain in depth of student understanding. We are convinced that the gain in depth is well worth the potential sacrifice of some breadth.

I. TEACHING LARGE CLASSES WITH ACTIVE LEARNING

Because large classes can be particularly prone to student passivity, instructors are required to find ways to refresh and actively engage students. Given limited student attention spans (often estimated as a maximum of 20 minutes), standing and talking or writing on the board for too long is a guarantee of losing the audience and this is even more likely the case with the increased anonymity a large lecture hall provides for students. Some faculty are able to use humor and personal stories to break and refresh a lecture. For the purpose of reengaging students, we propose using reinforcing and learning exercises that actually add to economic understanding and that are accessible to almost all faculty.

Although active learning techniques are becoming popular alternatives to straight lectures in many different environments, it is a common misconception that active learning techniques replace lectures. We suggest these techniques as tools for lecture enhancement, not replacement. Class size should not prevent an instructor from using innovative pedagogical techniques. As the instructor changes format moving from lecture, to discussion, to group work, student engagement is more likely to be maintained. Effective instructors can learn how to adapt the techniques to the larger setting and eventually begin to think of new techniques that cater specifically to large classes.

II. MOTIVATING STUDENTS IN EVERY CLASS

The sense of anonymity that students often feel in a large class strengthens the inclination to skip class or to tune out of the lecture when they do attend. Regularly graded activities such as quizzes, short writing assignments, and other exercises during class provide students with very persuasive incentives to attend class, pay attention, and get actively involved in learning.

If the instructor choses to give quizzes, the format can be very flexible. A quiz might cover the assigned reading for that day or the notes from the previous class period to encourage students to keep up with the material and be prepared for class. To provide incentive for attentiveness and involvement, a quiz might be given at the end of class that requires students to immediately apply or discuss newly presented material. Quizzes can facilitate group work by keeping group members focused if the end product of the group activity is an answer submitted as a quiz or short writing assignment. To make administration, collection, and grading of quizzes more manageable with hundreds of students, the instructor might have the question or questions on an overhead to avoid handing out paper and have students complete quizzes on index cards or computer bubble sheets, which are much easier to handle and process. The technology exists to give quizzes with objective questions and have those quizzes automatically graded and made available to students.

As in any group work, accurate and effective evaluation and reduction of potential free rider problems are challenges. A variety of methods has been used ranging from assigning relatively small portions of course grades to group work to asking students to grade the efforts or contributions of group members and using these grades as a part of individual student assessments. A colleague has used group projects in a large statistics course for years and identified free rider problems only a handful of times. His groups are small (two to three) and he assigns group work a relatively small part (for example, 10 percent) of the course grade. He forms groups by asking students for names of individuals they know and with whom they would like to work. Students without name suggestions are formed into groups at random. Those requesting changes are granted changes, but the frequency of such requests is negligible.[1]

Short writing assignments can also be a very effective tool in large classes. The instructor might leave students with a thought-provoking question at the end of one class period assigning a one-page response due at the beginning of the next class. This can serve as a good lead-in to discussion in the subsequent class period. The instructor might close a class period with a one-minute paper (Chizmar and Ostrosky, 1998) to see if students understand the material that was just presented by writing what is most clear and least clear. Such assignments encourage students to think about material during class, and provide students the opportunity to process their thoughts as they write. They provide the instructor with invaluable feedback about their understanding of the material. Chizmar and Ostrosky evaluated the use of the one-minute paper in which students were asked at the end of class about what they thought was 1) the most important point and 2) the most confusing point taught in class that day. They found that when comparing classes where this technique was used with those where it was not, there was a statistically significant increase in learning in classes using the one-minute paper.

It is not necessary to grade the content of all of these quizzes and short writing assignments. For some quizzes, writing assignments, or one-minute papers, the instructor might just give the students credit for completing the assignment. This will keep the workload more manageable and maintain incentives for students as long as there is uncertainty as to when grading will occur. Often in large lectures, grades are based solely on computer-graded exams. Most students appreciate having a portion of their grade based on activities that reflect attendance and effort. These quizzes and short writing assignments seem to foster attendance and attentiveness, encourage involvement in class, and eliminate taking attendance for its own sake.

Frank (forthcoming) discussed student grading and ranking of group and individual papers. His methods not only reduce his direct grading costs but seem to reinforce student understanding of analysis and the meaning of a good argument and discussion.

For both quizzes and short writing assignments, the instructor might sometimes ask students to work individually, sometimes in small groups, and sometimes to work alone and then form small groups to combine and improve their responses. Becker (2000) discussed the use of multiple-choice questions followed by small group and one-on-one discussions of the correct answers. The collaborative element fosters community in the classroom and generates more fruitful class discussion if the instructor afterward poses the question again to the class as a whole for discussion. The instructor can follow in-class quizzes and activities with some discussion so students not only are aware that these assignments are linked to credit toward their grade, but also know that they might be called upon to share their responses following the activity. This last element appears to increase the potential learning impact of the exercise.

III. TURNING LARGE CLASSES INTO SMALL ONES

A thoughtful lecturer may open with an outline of what the hour will bring, tell a story, lay out the theory in a careful, logical manner, summarize with insights or policy applications suggested by the theory, and close. An effective alternative, summarized in Table 5.1, is to begin the class with a short (7 to 10 minutes) lecture, demonstration, or story on a specific concept or topic. Two or three of these mini-lectures (perhaps two in a 50-minute class and three in a 75-minute class) followed by questions, discussion, and feedback will fill the entire class period. Following the lecture, a question is asked and students are given time to think about the answer and respond. The question can be shown on an overhead, a computer screen, or written on the board. For recording and feedback purposes, multiple-choice questions are most effective as students can respond with a show of hands.

The results are reported back to the students. If there is considerable disagreement about the correct answer, the students can be asked to talk to their neighbors about the correct answer. Easy questions (90 percent correct answers) create little interest and not much to discuss. The more difficult questions (20 percent correct answers) confound too many students for a productive interaction. The most encompassing and lively discussions seem to come from questions that result in about 50 percent of students selecting the correct answer.

After a few minutes of discussion, students are asked to respond again. Faculty or graduate teaching assistants record answers again. If there is no

TABLE 5.1: Format for Mini-Lectures

Activity		Time Allocation
Lecture, demonstration, or story		7-10 minutes
Ask multiple-choice question		1 minute
Time for students to think		1 minute
Respond and record		½ minute
Ask students to convince neighbors		1 – 2 minutes (if necessary)
Respond and record		½ minute
Explanation of incorrect and correct answers		2 – 5 minutes
	Total	13 – 20 minutes
Three activities per class	Total	39 – 60 minutes

convergence after the discussions, the instructor can eliminate options in the question or provide suggestions about how to solve the problem.

Instructors should be aware that a few students seem to respond slowly and are unable or unwilling to participate. They simply make note of the correct answer with the intention of thinking the question through at a later time. It may be that their learning styles support that type of study. However, it is just as likely that they have not prepared for class in a serious or effective manner, or that they do not yet know the material well enough to participate effectively.

The responses can be through a show of hands alone, or a show of hands and a written response to be turned in, or on handheld computers or remote devices available from a number of sources. Large cards labeled with letters for each option can also be held up by students.

Electronic personal response systems require that each student or small groups of students have a wireless responder. The classroom is equipped with wireless receivers linked to a computer. Student choices are entered on remote devices and the results for the class can be projected immediately in summary form. Results for each student are recorded and can be used for grading if desired.

Similar systems have been used in corporate training for some time. The same type of system can be used for in-class quizzes. However, beyond immediate feedback, it is not clear that there are significant advantages to such use of the systems. An advantage of electronic recording (or paper, but with more administrative challenges) is that when students are asked to respond, they are thinking. Every student in the class is being directly asked a question. Every student gets feedback and every student feels subtle pressures to participate seriously. The instructor gets immediate feedback on student understanding and has the opportunity to give additional attention to an issue, if appropriate.[2]

It is actually not hard to lead a traditional discussion in a large class. Typically there are enough aggressive, willing, and prepared students to discuss a case study, solve a problem, or apply a principle. Calling on students does not always work because of some students' fear of speaking in front of a large number of peers. However, asking questions and soliciting answers is often effective. It is a way of actively engaging the very best and most gregarious students and may be an alternative to lecturing as a method of demonstrating analysis to those who are less willing to participate. The problem is, of course, that you are leading a discussion among a relatively small portion of the entire class and are certainly contributing less to the rest of the class.

IV. GETTING STUDENTS TO LEARN FROM EACH OTHER

Students learning from each other as they work in small groups is often described as cooperative learning. "Collaborative learning" is used to mean the same or a somewhat broader pedagogy – "students doing things and thinking about the things they are doing" (Bonwell and Eison, 1991). Johnson, Johnson and Smith (1991) believe that cooperative learning may be effective in terms of achievement and has positive external effects on persistence, attitudes toward the subject matter and courses, and students' own abilities.

Although cooperative learning methods are most often used in small classes, they can also enhance instruction in large classes. Jigsaw, structured problem solving, and think-pair-share are three common types of activities.

Jigsaw

This strategy is particularly effective for issues and problems that can easily be separated into distinct parts. For example, fiscal policy might be broken down into changes in spending to affect demand, changes in spending to affect supply, changes in taxes to affect spending, and change in taxes designed primarily to affect supply. In a jigsaw activity, each group of three or four students focuses on a reading and discussion for one part of the problem. After developing an understanding among themselves, they discuss a way of communicating the issue to other students. Next each member of the group joins three others who have concentrated on their assigned issues. Students then introduce their part of the puzzle or issue to the new members of the group.

Evaluation of the activity can take place with a quiz at the end of the exercise or teaching assistants can judge the quality of the discussion and assign points. Alternatively, students can write small papers summarizing the results on a single page or card for evaluation.

Structured Problem Solving

In this approach students are put into groups of four and a brief lecture or handout introducing the problem is provided. Each student is assigned a number (1 through 4) within his or her own group. The group solves the problem in a way that they all agree and prepares so that any one of them can explain their analysis to others. After some period of time, the instructor randomly selects a number – say 3 – and student number 3 then presents his or her group's analysis to the class or to other groups. The method can be used effectively with brief case studies.

Think-Pair-Share

After a question or issue is presented to the entire class, students are given a minute to think about solving the problem or answering the question. Then students find a partner, usually the person sitting next to them in a large class. All students have the opportunity to think, share, and discuss the issue. The instructor then calls for a vote or individual comments. Students are much more likely to speak out because they now have a partner to support their answer. The responses are usually more thoughtful because of the time spent thinking through and discussing the problem.

Case Studies

All three of the above-mentioned cooperative learning approaches can be used with case studies. The case method presents real-world problems in which students are expected to apply economic concepts and principles with a pedagogical goal of better understanding the economics and developing abilities to recommend economic policy. The benefit of using case studies is in giving students practice in applying concepts and in thinking analytically about current social, political, and economic issues and problems. The primary challenge in large classes is to create significant rewards and incentives to participate.

Cases may be used effectively in a wide variety of formats. One of the easiest and most effective methods is to use a short case study as a distinct part of a class period. Such use provides an opportunity to involve students in applying the concepts or principles just discussed and breaks up the period into a more interesting class.

Small groups can be assigned the task of addressing different questions within the same case. The analysis can be formed by each group and then presented to the class as a whole. If each group is asked to do the entire case, class discussion and involvement will be best if, as is likely with cases involving controversial public policy, different conclusions or recommendations emerge. Alternately, each group can be assigned different cases to discuss in class. The small group discussion can occur either within class or outside of class with brief presentations made in class, and perhaps short papers turned in for evaluation. Cases can be used as exam questions or students can be asked to debate policy issues by assigning students to different sides based upon different interpretation of data, different applications of theory, or different goals. Debriefing is one of the most important parts of case studies (and for that matter, all active learning experiences). The instructor should devote as much or more time to the debriefing as to the activity itself.

Discussion Break

Another simple method of encouraging students to learn from each other can be as straightforward as scheduling a regular break in class to permit students to clarify with each other what their misunderstandings or confusions are. A three or four minute discussion break, particularly in the middle of a 75-minute class, can be refreshing. Students may be more willing to raise hands and say that they do not fully grasp an explanation when they know that they are not the only ones in the class with a question about a concept or topic.

V. USING EXPERIMENTS AND SIMULATIONS

A wide range of experiments and simulations have been created and tested in a variety of contexts. Depending on the design of the experiment, it may be that all students in the class can participate or it may be that only a subset can participate as the process and outcome are demonstrated for the entire class. In the latter instance, the instructor should not underestimate the effectiveness of the demonstration aspect of the activity for the students who do not participate. It still provides a very engaging and often entertaining format change for all students. Demonstrations can be quick and dramatic, such as when David Colander (and others) rips a twenty-dollar bill in half to show students that the value of money comes only because they think it is valuable. Even a simulation as simple as a production process showing diminishing marginal products engages the vast majority of students not participating in the simulation. The students who are participating might gain less that those watching their peers participate and perform. These types of demonstrations are often among the events students seem to remember for years to come.

The derivation of supply and demand curves in a class simulation gets the attention of almost all students and the active engagement of most as students think about how many apples or oranges (or movies) might be demanded at each price, and then think how many apples or oranges (or hours of labor) might be supplied at each price. A one-minute paper or a simple note written by the observers to explain why the results appeared helps to reinforce the basic concepts. Labor markets can be simulated by giving values of marginal products of a variety of types of labor to four or five firms, each with about four managers. Other students become the workers, and are given varying skill levels and varying appropriate marginal products.

If an instructor is considering more sophisticated classroom experiments, well-developed and documented experiments abound and their start-up costs are falling. There are many experiments in which students derive demand and supply and then equilibrium is determined through exchange. Modifications of this type of experiment can show the effects of taxes, externalities, and other factors influencing market outcomes. Sources include the work of Davis and Holt (1993), Kagel and Roth (1995), Bergstrom and Miller (2000), Friedman and Sunder (1994), Hazlett (2000), Keenan (1999), and many others.[3] Most of these sources provide explanations of how to effectively conduct the experiments, and more broadly show how they fit into the larger design of the course. Numerous experiments are also available from sources such as the *Journal of Economic Education* and *Classroom Expernomics.*[4] Experiments may also be conducted interactively online, both inside and outside of the classroom using one of many new websites such as Paul Romer's Aplia.[5] Most principles textbooks now include classroom experiments in the supplemental materials that are provided both in hard copy and online such as *Classroom Experiments: A User's Guide* (Delemeester and Neral, 1995), which accompanies John Taylor's principles text and *Experiments in Teaching and in Understanding Economics* (Ortmann and Colander, 1995), which accompanies Colander's principles text.

Carefully selected games and experiments can maintain student attention, emphasize relevance and help students discover economics as they do economics. However, instructors who adopt them should be mindful that start-up costs are not zero. Extensive classroom experiments can require substantial preparation and orchestration, to ensure that the expected gain in learning is sufficient to justify the incorporation of such activities.

Debriefing and discussion are again just as important, if not more so, as the actual experiment or simulation. If only a portion of the class takes a direct role in the activity, others can be assigned roles as observers and summarizers. Observers can be asked to submit brief written descriptions, interpretations, and conclusions of the activity. The direct participants may also be asked to summarize and discuss the meaning of what they just experienced.

VI. USING BRAINSTORMING

Brainstorming is an ideal way to begin a new section of material or to introduce a topic. For instance, on the first day of class the instructor could ask students what they think of economics or what they think the study of economics includes. This type of free association allows students to signal their attitudes about economics and gives the instructor some understanding of their prior knowledge. When beginning a discussion of monopoly students might be asked for their view of the pros and cons of a highly concentrated market. When talking about price discrimination, students might be asked to come up with all of the examples of price discrimination they have experienced first hand. In introducing economic growth, the instructor might introduce his or her family – for example, a man, a woman, and a dog – and ask for suggestions as to how to improve the family's well being in the future. These last three examples are not as much of a free-association brainstorming as the first, but they still require students to call upon their prior knowledge and think through their own opinions and ideas. Brainstorming gets students involved from the beginning.

In essence, most students will actively participate in the activity whether they respond aloud or not, as all find themselves thinking about what they would say. The instructor could ask each student to write their response on a card so all are formally active. During a brainstorming session, an instructor should acknowledge and record all student responses without comment or judgment. This is crucial in order to minimize the sense of threat students feel and to elicit a full range of responses from students. The discussion, organization, and evaluation of the responses can follow once all are heard or collected.

VII. CREATING A COURSE WEBSITE

Independent course websites or portals on classroom management systems provide opportunities for easy and accurate communication outside of the classroom. Many professors agree that putting the syllabus, daily announcements, and assignments online has benefits. Some argue that a course website provides a reliable resource for the many students who might miss a class on any day for legitimate reasons. The Internet can be an especially effective tool for maintaining order and mitigating confusion in a large class.

Opportunities for active learning are not found just in the classroom. Rather than only listing reading assignments, a course website can offer active learning possibilities. References and links to games or simulations that reinforce in-class concepts, practice exams, or daily quizzes with feedback can make outside reading assignments even more productive.

VIII. SUMMARY

Teaching a large class can be a daunting task. The best-planned, most logical lecture with a series of interesting stories and relevant examples often is met with blank stares from a substantial number of students. However, a class conducted in a large impersonal physical setting need not be devoid of interactive and intellectually stimulating learning experiences. In this chapter we have presented alternatives – the motivation for and advantages of active learning methods and described techniques that we find to be especially effective in our own large economics classes. From our experience we have found that these techniques increase the likelihood of engaging students, and enhance learning and enjoyment for student and instructor alike.

We close with advice to ensure the effectiveness of active learning in large classes and suggestions to enhance the overall experience for students in these classes. Successful instruction is possible in a large class; it only requires extra attention to techniques and planning on the instructor's part. With a skillful mix of classroom management and teaching techniques instructors can create an atmosphere conducive to learning and student involvement and effectively convey economic content in a large lecture hall setting.

IX. INCREASING LEARNING IN LARGE CLASSES: A DO LIST

- Do determine learning goals for the course and each class and select activities accordingly. Possible goals might be to teach a specific concept, reinforce or check the ability to apply a concept, measure student understanding, or allow students a chance for reflection and self-assessment. Activities should have learning benefits that exceed the costs of preparation, class time, and the potential reduction in overall content coverage. Gratuitous active learning efforts can backfire, so be judicious and decide if the selected pedagogical technique is the best way to present the topic at hand.

- Do provide very clear instructions for activities. Students will not understand what it is they are to do during the activities unless you have laid out clear guidelines. Remember, the general level of underlying confusion is naturally higher in a large class. Written instructions on paper or an overhead are much more effective than verbal directions. Instructions should briefly indicate the goal of the activity. Establish time limits to help students maintain focus. Incentives for participation and how students will be evaluated should be made obvious.

- Do write thought-provoking questions to use with activities. Construct questions with answers that are not obvious. Discussion will not occur if questions can be answered by a yes or no or with facts or repetitions of definitions. Higher-level questions will generate significantly more interest and discussion.

- Do create a comfortable classroom atmosphere that is conducive to active learning. Offer students advice for how to approach the class and active learning activities. Students who are comfortable in the classroom setting will more readily engage in activities. Demonstrate fairness by describing how you will deal with free riders.

- Do allow for adequate pre-class preparation time for activities. Consider that activities may require adjustments to adapt to the teaching space and available technologies in the classroom. The activity will most likely require distribution of instructions or other materials that must be prepared in advance.

- Do prepare for effective discussion. Even with well-planned active learning methods, a very large group of students is still undeniably an audience. A short lapse in the presentation, caused by lack of preparation, can lose the audience. Regaining lost attention is more difficult than just maintaining student attention. The instructor might incorporate some "planned spontaneity" into the lecture. Think of possible routes for junctures in the lecture that can go in one of several directions. Think of questions or ideas to interject that can jump-start a stalled discussion. In a large class setting the instructor cannot count on examples naturally emerging from students during discussion, and should prepare backup examples. If the instructor plans to tell a story to make a point, he or she must think it through in advance, anticipate various student reactions and plan how to respond to each one.

- Do start out small, then expand and personalize activities gradually. The newcomer to active learning should start out small. Low-cost/high-benefit activities to start with might include having students take two minutes to write a response to a question in class, then allowing two minutes to discuss their answers in "buzz groups" before the class as a whole discusses the answer. Active learning does not require an elaborate experiment that takes the entire class period to conduct. As an instructor develops a cadre of classroom activities, he or she can personalize the nature, emphasis, and length of the activities based on experiences, preferences and teaching style.

- Do know things about the audience such as interests, attitudes, prior experience, and knowledge. This will make the choice of active learning and other strategies and examples more effective. On the first day of class have students complete an information sheet. When selecting examples and articles choose items that will interest students, but at the same time have sufficient substance.

- Do have an active course web site. Use the website or course management system to give opportunities to students for active learning outside of the classroom. For example, self-quizzes with feedback provided after students have selected an answer provide opportunities for additional practice and feedback. Brief case studies based on current events or economic announcements or economic thoughts for the day may provide additional motivation.

- Do incorporate role-playing opportunities into the lecture. Role-playing can involve only a few students or committees of students backing up individual presentations. Students can be assigned roles of presidential advisers, members of Congress representing varying constituencies, labor, manage-ment, or resource owners. Students can be assigned roles at random. Although this can be very threatening, it is also a tremendous motivation for completing reading assignments. Some instructors find that allowing students to have some choice is a more productive approach. Students need time to prepare their roles – either prior to class, in a brief discussion within small groups, or simply with a few minutes of work alone. The assignment and descriptions of the roles should be clear enough to let the students know who they are supposed to be, perhaps with guidance provided as to what their positions on issues might be. Otherwise students may go off on tangents that take time and might lead the discussions in unproductive ways. A play with specific scripts, however, does reduce creativity and the opportunity for students to explore their own abilities to analyze and solve problems.

- Do incorporate examples and techniques from alternative sources such as literature. Although literature, drama, music, and poetry might seem out of place in economics classrooms, these are perhaps more effective than any other sources at capturing the attention of those students who claim to enjoy economics the least. An instructor might incorporate an example from classic literature such as the examples laid out in Watt's (2003) *Literary Book of Economics*, or have teaching assistants take on the persona of Adam Smith or Alan Greenspan and engage in dialog with students. Students can be also asked to create poems about economic topics.

X. INCREASING LEARNING IN LARGE CLASSES: A DON'T LIST

- Don't ignore students as they engage in group or individual activities. Use this time to walk around the room, observe students, and offer some guidance if deemed necessary for progress. If students think the instructor is not paying attention to them, some will be less likely to stay on task.
- Don't expect that recognition and understanding and factual questions will generate interest. Questions that involve students will be those that are challenging enough to merit discussion and thought. However, if they are too difficult, students will give up and there will be little basis for discussion.
- Don't skimp on the follow-up discussion. Use discussion and debriefing to reinforce the learning outcome of the activity. Much of the learning from an activity comes from helping students process the experience.
- Don't assign lengthy articles for cases or background where only a small part is relevant. This can waste student study time and make them doubt the relevance of the reading assignments. The result might be less preparation in the future.
- Don't assume an effective discussion can take place with no or little preparation on the student's part. Reward students for reading prior to class. Give questions to students as assignments are made. Ask students to outline or write out answers before coming to class. Provide questions for people to help them read actively instead of passively. Give estimated time to read an assignment.

NOTES

[1] Malcolm Getz in the Department of Economics at Vanderbilt University has used group projects in large economic statistics courses for more than a decade.
[2] Mazur (1997), who has done a great deal of evaluation of peer learning with physics students, argues in favor of devoting the entire class session to this format. Although that may be effective, we suggest doing some of the peer learning activity combined with a variety of other active learning experiences and lectures.
[3] For more classroom experiments, see Charles Holt's website at <http://www.people. wirginia.edu/~cah2k/teaching.html> and Denise Hazlett's website at <http://people. whitman.edu/~hazlett/econ/>.
[4] *Classroom Expernomics* can be found at <http://mcnet.marietta.edu/~delemeeg/ expernom.html>. This website is a resource containing noncomputerized economic

experiments that aid in teaching fundamental macro and microeconomic concepts. This website also contains a comprehensive list of links to additional economic experiments for the classroom.

[5] Paul Romer's Aplia may be found at <http://econ.aplia.com>. Use of the materials does require registration and a fee.

REFERENCES

Becker, W. E. 2000. Teaching economics in the 21st century. *Journal of Economic Perspectives* 14 (Winter): 109–19.

Bergstrom, T., and J. H. Miller. 2000. *Experiments with Economic Principles.* 2nd ed. Boston: Irwin McGraw-Hill.

Bonwell, C. C., and J. A. Eison. 1991. *Active Learning: Creating Excitement in the Classroom.* ASHE-ERIC Higher Education Report no. 1, George Washington University.

Chizmar, J., and A. Ostrosky. 1998. The one-minute paper: Some empirical findings. *Journal of Economic Education* 29 (Winter): 3–10.

Davis, D., and C. A. Holt. 1993. *Experimental Economics.* Princeton: Princeton University Press.

Delemeester, G., and J. Neral. 1995. *Classroom Experiments: A User's Guide*, written to accompany *Economics* by J. Taylor. Boston: Houghton-Mifflin.

———, eds. *Classroom Expernomics.* An electronic journal: <http://mcnet.marietta.edu/~delemeeg/expernom.html>.

Frank, R. H. Forthcoming. Testing for in-depth understanding in the economics principles course: The economic naturalist writing assignment. *Journal of Economic Education.*

Friedman, D., and S. Sunder. 1994. *Experimental Methods: A Primer for Economists.* Cambridge: Cambridge University Press.

Hazlett, D. 2000. An Experimental Education Market with Positive Externalities. *Journal of Economic Education* 31 (Winter): 44–51.

Johnson, D. W., Johnson, R.T., and Smith, K. 1991. Cooperative learning: Increasing college faculty instructional productivity. ASHE-ERIC Higher Education Report no. 4. Washington, DC: George Washington University.

Kagel, J., and A. Roth. 1995. *The Handbook of Experimental Economics.* Princeton: Princeton University Press.

Keenan, D. 1999. *Economics Live! Learning Economics the Collaborative Way.* 3rd ed. Boston: Irwin-McGraw Hill.

Mazur, E. 1997. *Peer Instruction: A User's Manual.* Upper Saddle River, N.J.: Prentice Hall.

Ortmann, A., and Colander, D. 1995. *Experiments in Teaching and in Understanding Economics*, written to accompany *Economics* by D. Colander. Chicago: Irwin.

Watts, M. 2003. *The Literary Book of Economics.* Wilmington: ISI Books.

CHAPTER 6

THE MACROECONOMICS PRINCIPLES COURSE: WHAT SHOULD BE DONE?

Peter E. Kennedy

The vast majority of students taking the principles of macroeconomics course will never take another course in macroeconomics. Indeed, with the exception of microeconomics principles, they will probably never again take any kind of economics course. They are taking macro principles because it is required of business majors, because it fulfills a breadth requirement, or because of general interest. Very few intend to major in economics, although we like to think that a good course will entice some students to rethink this decision.

Given that the macro principles course is our only chance to teach these students something about the macroeconomy, what should we do? Judging by the contents of our discipline's popular macroeconomics principles textbooks, it seems we believe that the answer to this question is "ensure that students are well prepared for intermediate macroeconomics courses by teaching them graphical analysis of macroeconomic thinking, and by covering a wide range of macroeconomic phenomena, terminology, and institutional detail." In contrast, this chapter is based on the premise that the answer to this question is "ensure that students remember a small number of important macroeconomics concepts, and know how these concepts can be used to make sense of the macroeconomics they are likely to encounter after leaving school." This view is not new. Hamermesh (2002, p. 449), for example, urged instructors to introduce "only those techniques that will be used in class in analyzing real-world issues: Teach ideas, not techniques. The purpose is to enable students to see economic principles in action in real life, not to prepare budding economics majors."

These different views about the purpose of our principles of macroeconomics course give rise to very different ways of teaching that course; the purpose of this chapter is to exposit how a macro principles course should be taught if the latter view is considered more appropriate.

I. RESISTANCE TO CHANGE

Instructors indoctrinated in the status quo are likely to raise several challenges to the view I have adopted above. These challenges, and the responses I have produced from related literature, from personal reflection, and from my teaching experience, form the foundation of this chapter.

- Surely we need to prepare our majors for the intermediate macroeconomics course by teaching them to manipulate relevant graphs? The answer to this is "yes and no." Graphs can be invaluable pictorial aids to students as the students explain how and why the macroeconomy reacts to a shock.[1] But going beyond this to push students to demonstrate by graphical means the details of their explanations does not pass a cost-benefit test. First, only a small fraction of the class will go on to the intermediate course. Second, they will have forgotten the graphical details. Third, instructors in the intermediate course, knowing they will have forgotten, will re-teach this material. And fourth, for students keen on majoring in economics these graphics are easy enough to pick up as they progress through the intermediate course.[2]
- Won't we be watering down the course if we abandon rigorous graphical or algebraic analysis? Changing the nature of the course may change the nature of the rigorous thinking involved, but need not change the level of rigor. Thinking like an economist requires clear, hard thinking, but not necessarily clear, hard thinking involving graphs or mathematics. Indeed, most students find my course difficult because it requires a different kind of problem-solving skill: an ability to take macroeconomics concepts and apply them to the real world, something students find very challenging. Consider, for example, the following news clip from Kennedy (2000b, p. 304): "Why has the governor of the central bank argued for a stable dollar and a zero inflation? Aren't these inconsistent goals?" Explaining why these goals are either consistent or inconsistent does not require technical expertise, but does require some clear, hard thinking along with an understanding of some basic macroeconomics concepts. How much easier if the question had been posed as follows: Explain why a country with a fixed exchange rate cannot maintain zero inflation if its trading partners do not have zero inflation.
- Aren't principles courses supposed to be survey courses, and so should cover a wide range of macroeconomics phenomena and terminology? The answer to

this, as is now widely recognized, is that less is more: It is far better to cover a small amount of important material well, than to skim over a large range of related material that will quickly be forgotten. Among economists, Saunders (1998, p. 91) expressed this view concisely: "It's not what you cover, it's what they learn. When instructors choose broad coverage, students end up familiar with but unable to apply the covered concepts."

- Shouldn't we at least ensure that students are familiar with economic institutions such as the Fed? Students should know what is the Fed, and how it operates to influence the macroeconomy, but do they need to know details such as the makeup of the FOMC, the names of key players, or the cities in which branches are located? The opportunity cost of imposing on students such soon-to-be-forgotten details is too high. This was an implicit message of Hansen, Salemi, and Siegfried (2002, p. 464) "The course fails because it does not teach students how to apply economics to their personal, professional, and public lives. The cost of jamming many topics into the course is that students never master the basics."

- Why are the most popular principles textbooks so encyclopedic? The main reason for this is that most textbook authors are trying to maximize sales, not student learning. See Dolan (1988), Stiglitz (1988), and Frank (1998) for an exposition of this and other reasons for this "market failure." According to Angelo (1993, p. 5) this character of our traditional principles textbooks flies in the face of research indicating that "One of the most difficult tasks for novice learners in a field, whatever their age, is to figure out what to pay attention to and what to ignore." Among economists, Boskin (1998, p. 27) had a cogent expression of this view: "The encyclopedia-like structure of most principles textbooks tends almost de facto to underemphasize basic economic concepts. ... However, the coverage of material in each chapter is often so extensive in the encyclopedia-like format that students have difficulty in determining which parts of the chapters are most important. In many cases, the side issues can be distracting or confusing for a large subset of the students."

- How do we determine the short list? Frank (1998, p. 13) asked exactly this question: "The best way to teach introductory microeconomics – or any subject, for that matter – is to expose students to repeated applications of a short list of the core ideas of the discipline. But *whose* short list?" In Frank (2002, p. 461) he answers: "The important thing is not which specific short list of core principles we try to teach, but rather that we have a well-articulated list of some sort and keep doggedly hammering away at it, illustrating and applying each principle in context after context." In an appendix to this chapter I have provided my own short list. According to Angelo (1993, p. 7), Frank's view has research-based support; it is one of Angelo's research-based principles for improving higher learning: "Learning to transfer, to apply previous knowledge and skills to new contexts, requires a great deal of practice."

- How can we ensure that students know how these concepts can be used to make sense of the macroeconomics they are likely to encounter after leaving school when we don't know what macroeconomics they are likely to encounter after leaving school? The main contact most students will have with macroeconomics after they leave school will be through media commentary.[3] By focusing the macro principles course on how to make sense of the macroeconomics found in the business pages of newspapers, a key element of this chapter, this goal should be achieved.[4]
- How can we ensure that students remember a small number of important concepts when they seem always to forget course content of whatever kind? Several means, discussed in this chapter, promote this kind of learning:

  1. Omit technical details if they are not crucial to understanding. Ensure that the big picture is clear. Avoid asking students to memorize things.
  2. Tell logical, verbal stories that describe how and why the economy reacts to shocks, rather than produce graphical or algebraic derivations.
  3. Use bold rules of thumb to reflect general results, rather than avoiding such rules because they are never quite correct.
  4. Connect to the real world by showing how the concepts discussed in class appear in the media.[5]
  5. Create challenging questions. Real learning occurs when the student hits his or her head against a problem designed to probe genuine understanding of important concepts.

The five items above reflect the remaining content of this chapter. A discussion of the role of technical details leads to a recommendation that we focus on verbal stories. I suggest that we adopt rules of thumb capturing key concepts. I provide a variety of examples of how media commentary can be integrated into the course and how it can be used to create challenging questions. Before concluding, I present a list of do's and don'ts implied by earlier discussions.

II. STORY TELLING

At the principles level most technical details do not enhance students' ability to apply the fundamental economic concepts we want them to learn. Why do students need to know the formula for the multiplier, or its graphical derivation (the 45-degree line diagram), for example?[6] All that is necessary is that they know the concept of the multiplier (that an increase in government spending can cause a greater increase in income), that they can explain how it comes about, and that they can apply this concept to real-world problems. Derivations of formulas and diagrams absorb student energy and so divert attention from the task of understanding.[7] Our focus should be on teaching students to tell a good verbal story[8] about how and why an economy reacts to a shock, rather than teaching how to analyze the economy's reaction to this shock algebraically or on a diagram. Colander (1995, p. 169) describes this eloquently:

> The economics we teach undergraduates is a combination of simple models with highly limiting assumptions and storytelling that relates the simple model to the economy. The models are comparative static: the storytelling generally fills in the missing dynamic analysis. At the introductory economics level, where the models are highly simplified, the storytelling grows in relative importance. A good principles of economics teacher is a good storyteller.

Doing this ensures that students can talk to laypeople (their parents?) about the forces that affect the macroeconomy, something that should be an important objective of the macro principles course. To do this the instructor has to create a straightforward dynamic adjustment path that avoids the messy everything-happens-at-once character of real-world economic adjustment, and present that path in a way that is pedagogically effective.[9] I use flowcharts for this purpose, mainly because I find that students can more easily assimilate a story through this medium than via a lengthy paragraph. This is because flowcharts display the entire adjustment process in a concise fashion, allowing students more easily to absorb the essentials of what is going on.

Consider the following example illustrating how a flowchart can display the operation of the Keynesian multiplier process:

$\uparrow$ G $\Rightarrow$ $\uparrow$ aggD for g&s
 $\Rightarrow$ excess aggD for g&s
 $\Rightarrow$ $\downarrow$ inventories, lost business, longer queues
 $\Rightarrow$ signal to firms [How react? $\uparrow$output? $\uparrow$ price? $\uparrow$ both?]
 $\Rightarrow$ $\uparrow$ output $\Rightarrow$ $\downarrow$ excess D
 $\Rightarrow$ $\uparrow$ income
 $\Rightarrow$ $\uparrow$ consumption demand
 $\Rightarrow$ excess demand, but smaller
 $\Rightarrow$ $\downarrow$ inventories and so repeat process

(Here $\uparrow$ means an increase in, $\downarrow$ means a decrease in, $\Rightarrow$ means leads to, and aggD for g&s means aggregate demand for goods and services.) A key step is the reaction of firms to the signal generated by the fall in inventories (or lost business, or longer queues for the service sector). This flowchart assumes an economy in recession and so follows a reaction that takes the form of an increase in output. When at full employment, an increase in price would be a more appropriate reaction. When incorporating the labor market, both price and output increases would be necessary. The important thing here is that this flowchart can be described in verbal terms, with the flowchart structure providing an overview of the process, facilitating understanding for students. This Keynesian multiplier process can now be used as an ingredient in subsequent analyses, as illustrated in the following example of an increase in the money supply.

Open market operations $\Rightarrow$ Fed buys bonds to $\uparrow$ money supply
$\qquad\qquad\qquad$ $\Rightarrow \uparrow$ price of bonds
$\qquad\qquad\qquad$ $\Rightarrow \downarrow$ interest rate
$\qquad\qquad\qquad$ $\Rightarrow \uparrow$ consumption, investment, and local government spending
$\qquad\qquad\qquad$ $\Rightarrow \uparrow$ aggD for g&s
$\qquad\qquad\qquad$ $\Rightarrow$ Keynesian multiplier process
$\qquad\qquad\qquad$ $\Rightarrow \uparrow$ income

Throughout the principles course students should be focused on the logic of the stories they tell, not the analytic details. Students at this level do not need to know how to derive the AD curve from the 45-degree-line diagram. Instead, they need to know only that if a higher price level decreases aggregate demand, equilibrium in the goods and services market requires a lower income level (indeed, one that is lower by quite a bit because of the multiplier process). Nor do they need to know how to manipulate the supply and demand for labor curves to show diagrammatically how different changes in wages and prices lead to temporary changes in output and employment. Instead they need to know only that a rise in price of 10 percent along with a rise in wage of 6 percent, say, will induce firms to hire more labor and myopic workers to supply more labor, creating a temporary upward slope to the AS curve. Nor do they need to know how to shift supply and demand curves on the foreign exchange market diagram to predict the direction of change of the exchange rate. Instead, they need to know only that certain factors such as changes in relative income levels, price levels, or interest rates will push demand for, or supply of, U.S. dollars on the foreign exchange market in certain directions and thus create excess demand or excess supply for U.S. dollars and so bid the exchange rate up or down.

III. RULES OF THUMB

As we know to our sorrow, there exist very few "laws" of macroeconomics. Market forces act automatically and virtually instantaneously to create an inverse relationship between the interest rate and the price of bonds, but beyond this it is difficult to find relationships that cleanly summarize important macroeconomic concepts. This is unfortunate, because summarizing key macro concepts via a "law" can be a useful anchor for students when learning these concepts. A compromise that I have found to be effective, described in Kennedy (1994), is to use "rules of thumb," which are technically not correct, but nonetheless in a summary sense capture the flavor of the macroeconomic forces in question.

Consider the example of determining inflation, for which I use the rule of thumb *inflation rate = money supply growth rate – real income growth rate.*

This rule of thumb results from telling a monetarist story based on the modern quantity theory of money in which the demand for money is a function of income. The essence of this story is that for equilibrium in the monetary sector, growth in money supply is matched by growth in money demand. Money demand grows because of real income growth and because of inflation, and this gives rise to the rule above. This result ignores a myriad of factors that could play a role here, such as money demand elasticities not equal to unity, interest rate influences on the demand for money, and banking innovations affecting the demand for money. Furthermore, this rule will be a poor predictor of inflation in the short run, as special features such as supply-side shocks and cyclical phenomena influence current price increases. In the long run, however, this rule should be a good guide to what is happening on the inflation front, something of which students can be convinced by graphing inflation against money supply growth for a range of countries, as shown in Figure 6.1. If advertised as a rule of thumb that provides a good prediction of what a country's inflation will be over the long run, it can provide students with an anchor capturing an important macroeconomic principle upon which, remarkably, most economists can agree: In the long run inflation is always and everywhere a monetary phenomenon.[10]

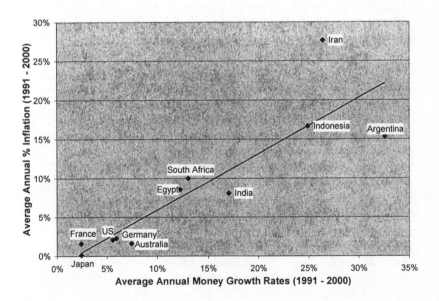

Figure 6.1: Inflation vs. money growth rates.

As a second example, consider the purchasing power parity (PPP) phenomenon, for which I use the rule of thumb

rate of change of the exchange rate = foreign inflation – domestic inflation.

This rule of thumb results from telling a story that begins "What would happen with a flexible exchange rate if our inflation were 5 percent higher than inflation in the rest of the world?" In the absence of exchange rate changes, the ever-widening gap between our prices and foreign prices should increase our imports and decrease our exports. The resulting balance of payments deficit should cause our exchange rate to be bid down. A fall of 5 percent per year prevents this disequilibrium from happening; forward-looking speculators in the foreign exchange market ensure that this will happen, giving rise to the rule given above. This result ignores a myriad of factors that upset this result in the short run, such as changes in interest rates and cyclical factors affecting exchange rates. And even in the long run this result is not reliable because of changes in the real exchange rate caused by things such as natural resource discoveries and changes in the terms of trade. But students can be convinced that this rule of thumb is a good rough guide to long-run behavior of the exchange rate by looking at what happens, over a decade, to the exchange rates of high-inflation countries, measured in terms of the currency of a single low-inflation country. A scatterplot plotting changes in exchange rates over a decade for several countries against their inflation rates during that decade, as shown in Figure 6.2, can illustrate the message of this rule of thumb.

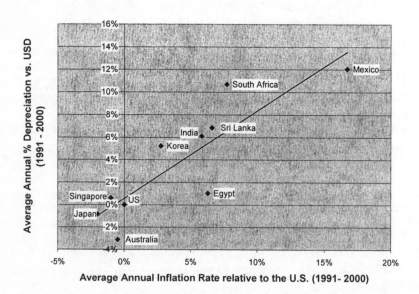

Figure 6.2: Exchange rate depreciation vs. relative inflation.

Both these examples have important policy implications. How should the central bank control inflation? Should the central bank adopt a monetarist policy rule or use its discretion? Does fixing our exchange rate have any implications for our inflation rate? Can fighting inflation be successful if we are unwilling to let our exchange rate rise? And both examples have important lessons for personal behavior. A rise in our money growth rate foretells higher inflation, which in turn implies a higher nominal interest rate and a fall in bond prices. We should sell bonds. A higher Mexican peso / U.S. dollar exchange rate may not mean a cheaper Mexican vacation; the rise in the exchange rate could have happened because of higher inflation in Mexico. So when we arrive in Mexico we may not find things cheaper (in our dollars) than during our previous Mexican vacation.

These rules of thumb present important macroeconomic principles in a form so stark that they cannot fail to make an impression on students. Two prerequisites should be evident, however, to ensure that this impression lasts beyond the course. First, a good story must be told to explain how these rules come about, and it must be made clear to students that they will be examined on their ability to tell this story in a clear fashion. This is to avoid the problem of students memorizing the rule of thumb without understanding the underlying economic rationale. Second, as the previous paragraph suggests, these rules of thumb carry with them substantive opportunity to connect to the real world; instructors should exploit this opportunity to impress upon students that what they are learning is of value for economic policy and of relevance to them personally.

IV. USING NEWS CLIPS

Connecting to the real world is the most effective way to convince students that what you are trying to teach them in your macroeconomics principles course is worth learning. Without this dimension your course will not motivate students to learn the material in a way that ensures it will be remembered after they graduate. Traditional textbooks try to accomplish this end by presenting examples of the real-world relevance of macroeconomic principles, but don't present enough of them, and, unfortunately, do not follow up with end-of-chapter questions based on real-world applications.[11] For example, earlier quotes from Robert Frank suggest that in his principles textbook (Bernanke and Frank, 2001) end-of-chapter macroeconomics questions would exhibit repeated applications of important principles, particularly in the context of examples drawn from everyday experience. But in fact a student encounters a truly alarming number of questions that begin "An economy is described by the following equations" and is asked to perform technical tasks, such as calculate the multiplier.[12]

Why have traditional textbooks failed in this regard? One reason is that they don't have room in their texts for many examples – they spend so many pages covering so many topics and so many details that they don't have enough room left over for examples. A second reason is that they tend to use examples that are lengthy (such as an entire newspaper article) using up limited page space. A third reason is that textbook writers tend not to put much priority on quality end-of-chapter questions – there are few questions, and they tend to focus on mechanical matters.

My solution to this failing is to use news clips, short one- or two-sentence excerpts taken from the business pages of the newspaper, as examples and as the basis for end-of-chapter questions.[13] This has several advantages. First, it is a direct connection to the part of the real world where students are likely to encounter macroeconomics after they graduate. Second, by using short clips, as opposed to complete articles, there is room for more examples. Third, more examples mean a greater range of applications can be presented. And fourth, because journalists tend to abbreviate expositions and write in language designed to impress readers, arguments are not spelled out as fully or as clearly as in textbooks. This creates a source of examples and questions that can influence student understanding far more effectively than the mechanical questions that characterize traditional textbooks.

A wide range of literature on the teaching of introductory economics stresses the need for examples that relate economics to students' personal experiences. An outstanding example of this is Frank (2002) who described this in terms of the "economic naturalist," someone who can use economics to explain everyday observations such as why airline meals are so bad or why the keypad buttons on drive-up automatic teller machines have Braille dots. One dramatic shortcoming of this literature, however, is that almost without exception the examples provided are microeconomics examples, with no mention of macroeconomics examples.[14] This is unfortunate because it suggests to instructors that good macroeconomics examples do not exist, with consequent negative impacts on the way in which introductory macroeconomics is taught. Certainly macroeconomics examples are not as close to students' everyday experiences as are microeconomics examples, but a perusal of Kennedy (2000a) should convince an instructor that plenty of macroeconomic applications are relevant to students' personal interests. Consider the following examples.

According to the latest statistics, housing starts are up, indicating unexpected strength in the economy. Bond prices fell on the news ... (p. 3)

In his eyes the battle is between the rate-lowering effect of the U.S. recession and the high rate of inflation. That sums up the problem now facing the interest rate forecasters. (p. 3)

News that U.S. job creation in January was more robust than anticipated sent a signal to currency markets to expect a stepped-up fight against inflation, unleashing a bout of buying fervor for the U.S. dollar. (p. 3)

These examples, typical of commentary on business pages in the newspaper, are of interest to students because they relate to money-making activity on bond or foreign exchange markets, or deal with variables such as interest rates that business people or mortgage renewers would be keen to forecast.

As with microeconomics, policy-oriented examples allow students to connect the material they are studying to the real world. Here are some examples.

What cannot be done, various reformers in the U.S. notwithstanding, is to impose on any government the obligation to balance its budget annually. Consider the consequences. If it did work, it would introduce a major destabilizing element. (p. 4)

The monetarists will allow you to go ahead and ruin people and countries but when eventually in good and common sense you say "enough is enough" the monetarists say "well, you spoiled the experiment." (p. 4)

This is the reason why the fixed exchange rate system was scrapped in 1971. The U.S. had been pursuing an inflationary monetary policy to help pay for the Vietnam war and new social programs, and its trading partners did not all want to participate in it. (p. 4)

Why would a balance-the-budget rule be destabilizing? What was the experiment and why was it spoiled? Why were U.S. trading partners unhappy? These questions are examples of how news clip applications can be challenging for students and truly test their understanding of important macroeconomics concepts, despite being nontechnical.

Kennedy (1992) identified five important macroeconomics concepts that appear prominently in the business pages of the newspaper, but which are not accorded comparable prominence in most principles textbooks.

1. **The discouraged/encouraged worker phenomenon.** The jobless rate fell to 7.5 percent last month, the lowest number in three years. But if you think it's a sign that the economy suddenly is moving up, look again.
2. **Using inventory behavior for forecasting.** When news of Wednesday's numbers on GDP was made public, the stock market immediately rose. Then, when analysis of the numbers came in, the market went into reverse – the greater part of the improvement in the quarter ($33.7 billion out of $39.2 billion) came from additions to business inventories.
3. **Money supply changes and the bond market.** A smaller than expected decrease in the U.S. money supply dealt the North American bond markets a hard blow, as bond prices sagged across a broad front.
4. **Inflation and the exchange rate.** In three to five years the U.S. dollar will presumably resume its long-term slide unless Washington reverses its economic policies of the post-Second World War period and takes a tough stand against inflation.
5. **Interest rate differences and the exchange rate.** Hart can't understand why Canadians would put their money in three-year paper at 9 percent when they can get double-A rated New Zealand bonds at 19 percent.

How could a fall in unemployment not be a sign that the economy is improving? Why would this inventory information cause the stock market to fall? Why did bond prices sag? Why would a tough stand against inflation stop the U.S. dollar slide? Why won't people invest in New Zealand bonds? These are the kinds of questions our students should be asked to work on, not derivations of algebraic equations or manipulations of graphs.

V. DO'S AND DON'TS

Several prescriptions follow from the discussion above, which I have supplemented with some suggestions from my own teaching experience.

- Do provide students with an overall picture of the structure of the macroeconomy.[15]
- Don't be encyclopedic. Realize that less is more; choose a list of important concepts and then make sure students learn those concepts well.
- Do tell straightforward verbal stories, summarized in a flowchart.
- Don't force students to learn how to derive graphs or know their technical details. Use the graphs only as visual aids to help students develop their verbal stories.
- Do use rules of thumb to capture the essence of important concepts.
- Do connect to the real world. The most effective way to motivate the average student is to demonstrate how what is being learned can explain real-world phenomena.
- Do provide several examples of how each important concept connects to the real world. Short, one- or two-sentence news clips are the most effective means of doing this.
- Do ask students to find for themselves news clips that are good examples of the macroeconomic concepts taught in your course. Such an assignment – identifying such news clips, and writing explanatory commentary on them – can be a useful learning experience.[16]
- Do create challenging questions to force students to think hard about how to use the concepts they are learning to explain real-world phenomena.[17]
- Do create challenging nonalgebraic, nongraphical questions that test understanding of theoretical concepts. Providing irrelevant information, or involving more than one concept, are ways in which questions can be made more challenging, and more realistic.[18]
- Do weight your exams heavily toward application questions and make sure students know this so they are motivated to do the work required to learn this dimension of the course.
- Don't dwell on technical details. The multiplier concept is important, not the multiplier formula, for example.

- Don't ask students to read a lot of material. Applications from the newspaper can take the form of short news clips rather than complete articles, for example.
- Do make the international sector an important part of your course. In the age of the global economy, understanding the international sector is crucial to interpreting macroeconomics in the news.[19]
- Don't teach the balance of payments as an accounting phenomenon, as many textbooks have a tendency to do. It is an equilibrium condition: the international sector of the economy is in equilibrium when the supply of U.S. dollars on the foreign exchange market equals the demand for U.S. dollars on the foreign exchange market, a zero balance of payments.
- Do explain the mechanics of bond prices. The inverse relationship between the interest rate and bond prices is a major macroeconomic concept with a direct connection to investor success (and so it is of potential personal interest to students), drawing daily commentary in the business pages of the newspaper.[20]
- Do pay special attention to the real versus nominal interest rate difference. It is the macroeconomic concept that contributes most to understanding macroeconomic commentary on the business pages of the newspaper.[21]
- Do consider beginning your course with the simple Keynesian model, rather than with the traditional discussion of measuring GDP, the price level, and unemployment. Measurement issues are important, but are not representative of the rest of the course; begin by hooking students on an interesting topic.

VI. CONCLUSION

Marks and Rukstad (1996) argued in favor of using case studies to teach intermediate macroeconomics. Case studies are not appropriate for the principles level, but much of the flavor of case studies can be imparted through the use of short news clips as advocated in this chapter. Borrowing from Marks and Rukstad (1996, p. 139), much of the message of this chapter can be summarized as follows. If we deny students the richness of news clip examples, we do them, and the macroeconomics profession, a great disservice. We do them a disservice because we withhold knowledge that only such real-world examples can convey. We do them a disservice because we withhold skills that most students could use in favor of skills most will never use. We do them a disservice because we present economics as dull, dismal, and lifeless when, in fact, it demands attention, grabs headlines, and profoundly inspires both our history and our everyday life.

A main thesis of this chapter is that we need to change the content/flavor of our macroeconomics principles course, toward a course that focuses on a small number of important concepts and then applies those concepts over and over to real-world examples so that students will learn those concepts well and remember them for use in later life. Frank (2002, p. 460) had an optimistic view:

The encouraging news is that we are in the early stages of a revolution in the teaching of introductory economics. Recently published texts, for example, tend to be shorter than the ones they displace, and also less ambitious in their breadth of coverage. Revolutions of this sort often proceed in small increments, however, and this one is far from running its course.

This chapter is a contribution to this revolution, supplying strategy and ammunition for the battle on the macroeconomics front.

APPENDIX 6.A: A Macroeconomic Principles Short List

Creating a short list of important macroeconomics concepts on which to base a principles course is a challenging task because so many macroeconomics ideas are important that any one person's selection of a few as "really important" is bound to be controversial. The first step in creating such a list is to address the question "Really important for what?" The list below stems from my answer, "Really important for understanding media commentary on the macroeconomy." It includes ideas important to those interested in how macroeconomics is relevant, ideas that students should be sure to understand and take with them when they complete their course. Because of this criterion, some of this short list departs from what traditional macroeconomics principles textbooks emphasize. For example, as I have argued elsewhere (Kennedy, 2000a), the macroeconomics concept that is most valuable in interpreting macroeconomics appearing in the newspaper is the distinction between real and nominal interest rates.

1. **Gross Deceptive Product.** Gross domestic product, GDP, figurehead of our national economic accounts and the measure of our total annual output of goods and services, has many defects as a measure of our economic well-being or as a means of comparing standards of living across countries.
2. **Discouraged/Encouraged Workers.** Unemployed people who become discouraged by their unsuccessful search for work, and therefore stop searching, are suddenly no longer counted as unemployed. When the economy picks up, they can become encouraged and begin looking for work again, thus becoming counted as unemployed. This discouraged/encouraged worker phenomenon helps explain paradoxical movements in the measured rate of unemployment and is an example of the more general problem of difficulties in measuring economic variables.
3. **The Multiplier.** An increase in government spending can ultimately cause a greater increase in national income. This multiplied impact of fiscal policy is one basis for the Keynesian view that the government can and should intervene in the operation of the economy to maintain full employment, even if it implies creating a budget deficit.
4. **The Natural Rate of Unemployment.** The institutional structure of an economy gives rise to a "natural" rate of unemployment toward which the

economy gravitates, consistent with a steady rate of inflation. Unfortunately, the natural rate is neither known, nor constant over time. In the mid 1990s it was thought to be about 6 percent, but because in the late 1990s inflation did not appear as the unemployment rate fell, most economists have revised this figure to below 5 percent. An important implication is that efforts to lower unemployment below this natural rate can succeed only in the short run and only by accelerating inflation.

5. **Productivity.** In the long run, increases in our economic standard of living depend primarily on productivity increases. To achieve higher growth in productivity we must increase national saving: present generations must sacrifice current consumption to improve productivity for future generations. Productivity increases often come about through "creative destruction," a process in which existing jobs are destroyed through the creation of new jobs embodying technological advances.

6. **Printing Money.** The U.S. central bank, the Federal Reserve Bank (the Fed), "prints" money by buying bonds, enabling commercial banks to increase their loans and thereby expand the nation's money supply. Irregular relationships between economic activity and measures of the money supply create problems for monetary policy.

7. **Inflation and Money-Supply Growth.** In the long run, an economy's inflation is equal to the difference between the rate of growth of its money supply and its rate of growth of output. This reflects the monetarists' belief that, in the long run, inflation is always and everywhere a monetary phenomenon, which leads to their prescription that the Fed should be replaced by a robot programmed to increase the money supply at a low, steady rate, the genesis of the prominent "rules-versus-discretion" policy debate.

8. **Interest Rates and Bond Prices.** A genuine economic "law" is that there is an inverse relationship between the interest rate and the price of bonds. One implication of this law is that if the interest rate is forecast to rise, those holding bonds will try to sell them to avoid suffering a capital loss.

9. **Real versus Nominal Interest Rates.** The interest rate affecting aggregate demand is the real interest rate. The observed interest rate – the nominal interest rate – differs from the real interest rate in that it has a premium for expected inflation built into it. For practical purposes, the main determinant of change in the nominal interest rate is change in the expected rate of inflation. This difference between real and nominal interest rates helps explain many seeming anomalies, such as an increase in the money supply causing a rise rather than a fall in the interest rate.

10. **Inflation Asymmetry.** Inflation accelerates quickly, with only a small temporary reduction in unemployment below its natural rate, but lowering inflation requires an extended period of high unemployment, primarily because it takes so long for expectations of inflation to fall. It is this asymmetry that causes governments to fight inflation so tenaciously.

11. **Monetary Policy Lost under Fixed Exchange Rates.** When a small economy fixes its exchange rate with a large economy, monetary policy must

maintain the exchange rate, and so cannot be used for other goals, such as controlling inflation. The small country must experience whatever monetary policy and inflation characterizes the large country.

12. **Purchasing Power Parity.** Although changes in our real exchange rate occur because of phenomena such as natural resource discoveries, in the long run movements in our nominal exchange rate primarily reflect differences between our inflation rate and the inflation rates of our major trading partners. One implication is that a country with higher inflation than its trading partners should experience a steady depreciation of its nominal exchange rate.

13. **Interest Rate Parity.** Save for a risk premium, real interest rates tend to be approximately equal throughout the world, but nominal interest rates are not. The latter differ according to inflation rate differences or, equivalently, to expected exchange rate movements. One implication is that a country with a nominal interest rate below that of its trading partners should be experiencing a continual rise in its exchange rate.

ACKNOWLEDGMENT

* My thanks to Christine Amsler, Lee Hansen, Michael Salemi, Bill Scarth, and Nic Schmitt for critical comments.

NOTES

[1] Although graphs can be invaluable pictorial aids, worth more than a thousand words, the empirical evidence does not show that they enhance learning; see Cohn et al. (2001).

[2] Marks and Rukstad (1996, fn. 9) argued cogently that technical material is not necessary even at the intermediate level.

[3] A European colleague has informed me that in Europe, compared to North America or Asia, people distrust "markets" and by extension economics, and are drawn to broader economic issues such as globalization, development, and IMF programs. If this is true, my examples, taken mainly from the business pages of the newspaper, should be supplemented with examples taken from other sections of the newspaper, such as the editorial page.

[4] This is not a novel suggestion. Boskin (1988, p. 158) wrote "In brief, I set as my goal helping my students to achieve mastery of enough simple analysis and descriptive overview that they can read the newspaper intelligently and critically." Hansen, Salemi, and Siegfried (2002, p. 468) noted that "Students should come away understanding that economic principles can explain important world events. Instructors should use recovered time to show how fundamental economic concepts can help explain issues covered by the *Economist, Wall Street Journal, New York Times* ...." Krueger (2002, p. 476) stated "I think it makes an infinite amount of sense to try to reach students by using current events and news articles."